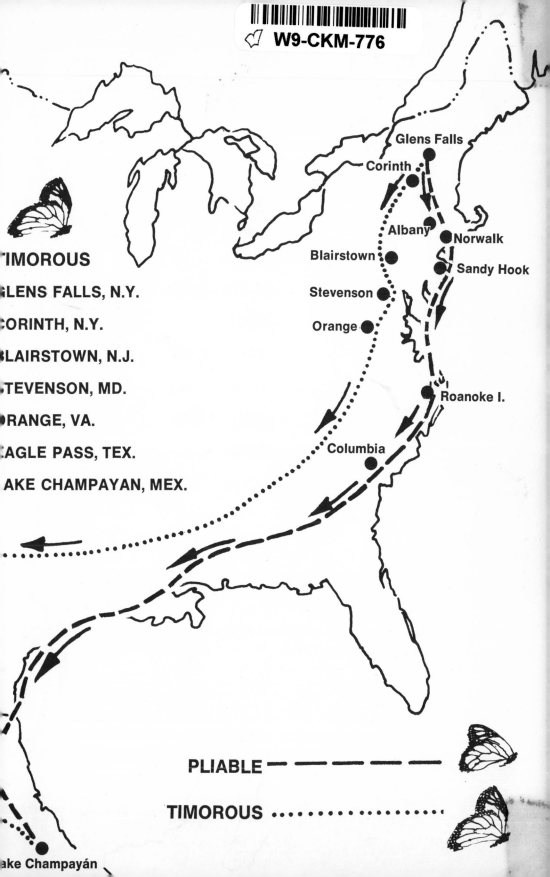

TIMOROUS

GLENS FALLS, N.Y.

CORINTH, N.Y.

BLAIRSTOWN, N.J.

STEVENSON, MD.

ORANGE, VA.

EAGLE PASS, TEX.

LAKE CHAMPAYAN, MEX.

Glens Falls

Corinth

Albany

Norwalk

Blairstown

Sandy Hook

Stevenson

Orange

Roanoke I.

Columbia

PLIABLE — — — — —

TIMOROUS ••••••••••••••••

Lake Champayán

THE YEAR OF THE BUTTERFLY

ALSO BY GEORGE ORDISH
The Great Wine Blight

GEORGE ORDISH

THE
YEAR
OF
THE
BUTTERFLY

Drawings by Thomas O'Donohue

CHARLES SCRIBNER'S SONS · NEW YORK

To Linda Grobstein

CONTENTS

CONTENTS

PREFACE

In Victor Scheffer's book *The Year of the Whale,* the reader is constantly amazed at the enormous weights and sizes involved, which some, myself included, found it almost impossible to visualize. In this work the opposite situation prevails: it deals with the very small which may be equally or even more difficult to appreciate. The book really should be approached with a magnifying glass in the brain, so to speak. It is constantly dealing with thousandths of an inch and thousandths of an ounce. Whereas Dr. Scheffer starts his story with a newborn whale calf weighing a ton, I begin with a newly hatched caterpillar weighing less than a thousandth of an ounce.

As new Gullivers let us hope to find Lilliput as interesting as Brobdingnag, for both the small and the large show the wonderful ways in which life exploits particular environments, extracting the maximum advantage from prevailing conditions.

The monarch butterflies make a fantastically complicated

journey, overcoming difficulties all the way along. Their progress is reminiscent of John Bunyan's great book, and consequently the protagonists, needing a steadfastness equal to Christian's, have been named after characters in *The Pilgrim's Progress*—Pliable and Timorous. The viceroys, Lady Feigning and Two-tongues, which play a part in the story because of their resemblance to monarchs, have been named from the same source.

Because Pliable and Timorous develop and travel at different rates, there is some necessary overlapping in the dates at the chapter openings, which are inclusive of the chapter content. A detailed chronology appears at the back of the book.

I thank many people for help with this work, particularly librarians of the New York Public Library, the Rothamsted Research Station (England), the Royal Entomological Society (London), and the Smithsonian Institution (Washington, D.C.); also J. Bleasdale (Wellington, Somerset, England), Marjorie Byers (St. Albans, England), E. J. Eames (London), Olive Moran (London), Sylvia Salem (Rome), C. J. Johnson (Jamaica, West Indies), Jack and Linda Grobstein (Long Island, New York), John Schlebecker (Washington, D.C.), and Janet Wurtzburger (Stevenson, Maryland), among others. Finally, I am grateful to my wife for her help in the construction of the book and the revision of the text.

THE YEAR OF THE BUTTERFLY

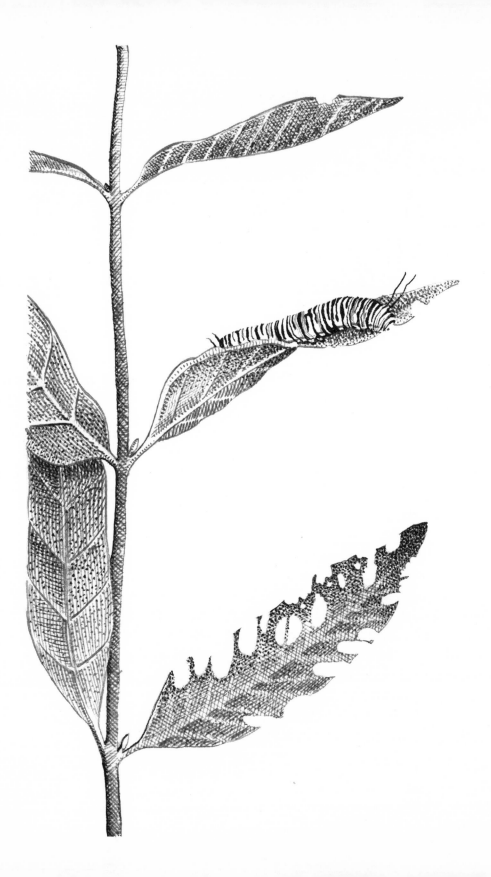

1 CATERPILLARS IN A MILKWEED PATCH

AUGUST 8 – 29

Plants of one kind or another are the source of all life and animals are the enemies of plants; they eat them. Plants fight back. Thorns are produced to protect the leaves against hungry mouths. Trees may produce their foliage high up on a long trunk to save it from large browsing animals, or a plant may produce poisonous or bad-tasting substances which will cause such animals to leave it alone. The milkweed and the yew tree are common examples, their foliage being bitter and poisonous to most mammals. But animals as a whole do not passively accept this situation; where there is a considerable quantity of food available some form of animal life able to exploit it tends to arise. In the natural world a food niche does not long remain vacant. The donkey and the camel can eat thorny foliage. Giraffes with their long necks can reach up to high leaves, and some animals, particularly insects, feed on leaves poisonous to the majority of

3

creatures. The caterpillar of the monarch butterfly finds the "poisonous" milkweed absolutely delicious.

On August 8 of a recent summer, in a patch of milkweed plants growing on waste ground by a gas station on a country road near Glens Falls, New York, a number of small creamy yellow objects, about the size of a pin's head, could be seen on the undersides of the young leaves. They were the newly laid eggs of a monarch butterfly and they were firmly secured to the leaf by a strong cement. The newly laid eggs were a light cream color at the base, merging into white at the top, and under a hand lens or low-powered microscope resembled an exquisitely carved Fabergé jewel. They were shaped something like an acorn and showed a series of about twenty-five ridges running from a circular base to a conical, blunt-pointed top. Between the ridges were a number of four-sided facets, making about thirty-four transverse circular rows parallel to the base. At the top a fine network pattern covered the micropyle, or sperm admission point, of each egg. A monarch egg is a beautiful object: within it a vast amount of biological activity ensues. Inside one of these fertilized eggs the male and female cells, or gametes, have fused to form a zygote which will grow to become the embryo. At first the zygote simply multiplies its cells as each daughter cell reproduces itself, leading to a small undifferentiated body of nearly identical cells. Then simple multiplication ends, differentiation starts, and the larva gradually forms in the yolk of the egg, on which it feeds.

The germ band then begins segmentation and the forming of the basic structures of the future insect; among the first seen are the ganglia of the central nerve cord, the cord itself, and the rudimentary head. The differentiation continues, the embryo still drawing food from the yolk and frequently shifting its position within the egg (blastokinensis) . All this goes on inside the shell and cannot be seen from outside. Of course the egg is very small; it measures about 20/1000 inch in diameter and 30/1000 inch in height. Its weight is about 2/100,000 of an ounce.

The milkweed patch by the gas station was not there by chance; it was being encouraged by the son of the station's owner. This young man, as a boy of twelve, had been given some old books by a neighbor, the widow of a minister. Among them were two by the late-nineteenth-century New England entomologist Dr. H. S. Scudder, who was among the first to study the monarch butterfly, and whose works are still an accurate source of information on the creature.[1] The boy's interest was aroused by the curious fact that certain insects fed on plants that were poisonous to men and mammals—crotons, poison ivy, milkweed, among others. Scudder had also observed that monarch caterpillars, which avidly consumed the leaves of most milkweed plants, avoided the variety called poke milkweed. Evidently the poke milkweed has developed in its fight for survival a substance which makes its leaves distasteful to the monarchs. Other insects also feed on milkweed; it is interesting that several of these in addition to the monarch butterflies are conspicuously colored.[2]

Inspired by his reading, the boy began observing monarchs for himself and though he had no training as an entomologist his interest continued and in time he started to breed monarchs on the milkweed patch by the gas station and to watch them carefully. His project attracted the attention of his customers, especially a girl from Albany who was studying entomology at Cornell University. She brought his ideas on monarchs up to date, and as their friendship developed, the two started experimental

5

work together, cultivating the milkweeds in the patch and
breeding the butterflies in a small shed which became in effect a
laboratory.

As the particular eggs already described continued to mature,
they became pearly in color. Leaden-colored spots, moving about
from time to time, could be seen through the semitransparent
shells. The spots were the black feet and head of the tiny caterpillar
within. In one egg the black marks extended, and the creature
inside began rasping the transparent eggshell near the top. It
paused to rest from time to time to let the chitin of its mouth
parts harden and become more effective; then it renewed the attack
on the shell. Chitin is the hard, tough yet elastic, waterproof main
constituent of the insect's external skeleton.

Eventually the larva managed to make a longitudinal slit in the
eggshell a few ridges below the cap. It paused a moment and then
pushed its head through the slit. A quick look around the new
world presented to it so suddenly seemed to arouse the creature's
interest, and pressing from side to side it soon squeezed out of the
shell and crawled onto the downy leaf. This happened on August
10. Nearby, on other leaves, other monarch eggs were hatching
into the warm sunlight—the warmer it is the quicker they hatch.
Some of the emergent larvae, however, did not appear to be as
enchanted with their surroundings as the first was, for after
emergence the head was pulled back and the little creatures
waited within the eggs, apparently resting to obtain strength and
courage for their forthcoming ordeal. Unlike the higher animals,
most young insects are thrust into the world on their own with no
parental care at all. Only a few kinds, such as earwigs, bees, and
wasps, so much as see their young, let alone look after them.

In order to follow the fortunes of two of these monarch larvae

6

it is well to give them names. The first to emerge will be called Pliable and one of the later ones Timorous, after the characters of these names in Bunyan's *Pilgrim's Progress*.

When Pliable, a female, got out of the egg she paused a few seconds, turned round, and then ate most of the eggshell, leaving only the solid base which was securely gummed to the leaf. At this stage she was about 94/1000 inch long and difficult to see. She turned quickly from the egg and moved about half an inch over the leaf, where she started to feed on the downy hairs of the leaf surface, clearing a tiny patch of leaf as she did so.

On the other hand, Timorous, a male, was among those that appeared reluctant to leave the comfort of the egg. Eventually he did so, later in the same day on which Pliable had hatched, and moved slowly away. Every now and then he raised the forward segments of his body and swayed from side to side, as if to get a view or smell of the landscape before him (an inch or so of milkweed leaf) and then moved slowly back to the egg to chew a bit of the shell.

This soft, minute creature, uncared for by a parent, was remarkably susceptible to accident and enemy. If he fell off a leaf he was unlikely to be able to return. If he wandered into a drop of water he would not have enough strength to overcome the surface tension and release himself. Numerous animals might eat him, but he was protected to some extent from birds by his tiny size and his position on the underside of a leaf.

Timorous moved away from his half-eaten eggshell to a fresh part of the leaf, again raising and jerking his head on the way in order to intimidate predators. A spider was frightened away, and an ant scout and a lizard just missed finding the small creature. Luckily for him no more spiders were around at that particular moment. He next started to eat a few more leaf hairs in

7

another part of the leaf. He soon left these, wandered on, and by an unusual chance came across another monarch egg, which he at once proceeded to eat. It is seldom that two eggs are found on the same leaf. The female monarch, after laying an egg, "marks" the leaf with a warning substance that causes other females to leave such labeled foliage alone. Fortified by the best part of two eggs, Timorous was able to tackle his leaf patch with an energy belying his name; he soon gave up feeding on leaf hairs and began to gnaw a hole right through the leaf to the upper surface.

Pliable was a bit more adventurous; she too had difficulty in traveling over the leaf hairs but was soon at work eating out a small patch about the size of a pin's head. She then turned, wriggled away, and started another patch. Always active, she returned from time to time to the first patch, enlarged it and then, with more food in her than Timorous had, started to eat the body of the leaf itself more vigorously. Before going through the leaf she twisted back again, visited one of the other patches she had cleared, and ate through that. She did the same with two more patches. They were all close together—that is, within a circle ¼ inch in diameter. The leaf now showed the sure sign of a monarch caterpillar's having started to feed: the appearance of several pinhead holes through the leaf quite close to each other. Pliable journeyed from one to the other, feeding a little at each place, and finally enlarged her original hole and squeezed through to come out on the upper surface.

At night the temperature dropped and both caterpillars stopped feeding. By August 12 the more active Pliable had begun to change color a little, from white to grayish; a black ring had developed around the base of her rudimentary antennae, or feelers. The black of the head had deepened, become shiny, and spread to the base

8

of the mouth parts. Timorous's development was a little slower and with him the change took place on August 13.

An insect is divided into three parts, and this is the reason for the name—it means "cut into" in Latin. The three sections are the head, thorax, and abdomen. True insects have six legs, and for this reason the class Insecta is also known scientifically as Hexapoda, from the Greek word meaning "six-footed." Spiders and mites are not insects, because they have eight legs and only two divisions of the body. Insects, spiders, mites, centipedes, crustaceans, and some other creatures belong to the phylum Arthropoda, which consists of jointed limbed animals. The six true legs of an insect are carried on the thorax, a pair each on the forward section (prothorax), the middle section (mesothorax), and the backward section (metathorax). Caterpillars also have false legs behind the true legs. There are usually five pairs of these, but the members of one family, the Geometridae, have only the last pair, the anal clasper, which is very useful for holding on to a leaf edge, twig, or other small object.

Caterpillars clearly show the structure of insects, which consists basically of chitinous rings, joined together and bearing the limbs and antennae. The creatures have no backbone, but an "exoskeleton," or hard flexible cover, to which their internal organs are attached.

Both Pliable and Timorous put their true and false legs to good use in holding tightly to the leaves and squeezing back and forth through the holes they had made in them. The insects fed voraciously, both to secure growth and to maintain pressure within the body cavity. Their outer skin started to stretch. Longish hairs were more apparent on their heads, which had four pairs of simple eyes, or ocelli. Their mouths were elaborate, consisting of two pairs

9

of jaws of hardened chitin, one pair working horizontally and an outer pair working up and down outside as the human jaw does. They made a considerable sound when feeding, as they took a number of short sharp bites followed by a pause: crunch, crunch, crunch—pause—crunch, crunch, crunch, crunch—pause. The sound is not audible to the unassisted human ear but most impressive when amplified from a microphone pickup.

It is possible to hear insects feeding with the unaided ear if there are enough of the creatures about. A swarm of locusts, settled on an orange grove on a still, warm night, can be heard very distinctly as they hungrily feed away. "Crinkle, crinkle, crinkle," go the jaws, with a sound of rustling as the insects move among the leaves. Every now and then there is a crash as a bough breaks under the weight of locusts on it; the insects flutter around a bit but are soon busy eating again, and the whispering "crinkle, crinkle" once more fills the air. Similarly, on a still day or night, caterpillars of the white cabbage butterfly can be heard feeding if their attack on a field of cabbages is severe enough.

Pliable and Timorous soon began to show the characteristics of their species. On the prothorax, in addition to the first pair of legs, was a pair of dark, triangular markings bearing some long hairs, and also a pair of breathing pores, or spiracles, protected by two long hairs (as are human noses, but with a larger number). Other sections of their bodies also had breathing pores; they do not breathe through their mouths. The prothorax hung down like a dewlap in front of the first pair of legs. The mesothorax carried the second pair of legs and on top of this part was a pair of fleshy projections, grayish in color, each carrying a hair at the end; these were to become an important feature of the fully grown caterpillars. A number of small swellings carrying hairs also developed on the mesothorax. The metathorax carried the hind pairs of legs; this segment had a longish darker area with four long hairs.

After two and three days, respectively, of eating and developing, the caterpillars' skins were stretched to bursting point. Pliable and Timorous were approaching the second great crisis in their lives. The first was hatching from the egg; the second, their first molt.

It has already been mentioned that insects have a hard, leathery, external skeleton; this hardly stretches at all. They cannot grow as vertebrates do, by extending the bones and adding more flesh, but must discard their entire envelope and substitute a new one beneath it. In fact, the caterpillar simply bursts out of its old skin. This process is more fully described later; here it need be noted only that the caterpillar rests, the old skin splits, and the creature makes tremendous efforts to wriggle out. This is a dangerous period on two counts. First, the insect is defenseless against predators. At this point a roaming ant or spider can easily snap it up. Second, the creature may not be able to free itself from the old skin. A chance thread, a sticky spot, or a bad position may relentlessly trap the caterpillar halfway out of its old skin; caught, the young insect sways, struggles, exhausts itself, and dies. This was the fate of many of the caterpillars on the patch of milkweed, but first Pliable and then Timorous, a day later, molted successfully. When they had emerged, air was absorbed and blood pumped into the new limbs and segments to increase the size of the insect in its second instar, which is what the period after the first molt is called. (The first instar is the period between hatching and the first molt.)

Once again Pliable was quicker and more active than Timorous. On emerging she rapidly inflated her body, turned and ate the old skin, stretched and tried her new limbs, and turned to enlarge the holes she had started in her leaf. Her markings and shape were now a little different. The solid, shiny black of the head was

11

broken by the appearance of two yellow stripes which left a black triangle beneath them. The black patch on the prothorax was longer and a black band was starting to form by the spiracle. The legs carried by this section were now smaller than those on the other thoracic sections and this forward pair had moved closer to the head. Many of the long hairs present during the first instar had now gone. On the middle thoracic section the projection noted in the first instar had increased in size and sprang from a band of darkish color now forming around the insect. The surrounds of the spiracles were also darkening. Generally the caterpillars appeared fatter in this stage than in the first instar. Other features of the second-instar caterpillars were the increased size of the filaments on the mesothorax and the appearance of some bands of color on the body.

The caterpillars started feeding yet more vigorously and rapidly put on weight. Most of the leaf on which Pliable had been born and had cast her first skin had been consumed. She moved to the stem of the plant, climbed to the next leaf up, and started feeding on it. Five minutes later this leaf too had been reduced to a skeleton and she moved on again to another young leaf. Timorous tried to do the same, but as he was about to move from the leaf to the stem a gust of wind shook the plant and threw him to the ground. The fall itself was not serious, because he was too light in weight to come to any harm, but he would be in grave danger if he did not soon find another milkweed plant, since his feeding habits were so highly specialized that no other food would do. When he fell Timorous remained perfectly still, shamming dead, so as not to attract the attention of predators such as birds and spiders. After a while he moved away, found a milkweed plant, for there were many growing in the patch, climbed up to near the top, and started feeding again.

After three days of this active life most of the caterpillars on
the milkweed patch were ready to molt a second time. They rested,
in due course the old skin split, and most of the newly clothed
insects emerged for the third time, among them Pliable on August
14 and Timorous a day later. Again they rested after their
Herculean efforts but were soon feeding again, building up the
tissues for the next stage. In this third instar they looked like an
enlarged version of the second. The filaments were slightly longer
and aligned along the back. The pigmentation was a little more
pronounced, and spots of darkish color, with short hairs sprouting
from them, appeared here and there. Again they fed avidly, for
a longer period in this instar. Pliable took six days (to August 20)
and Timorous seven days (to August 22). They both sought safe
places, rested, and molted for the third time into the fourth-instar
stage.

In the fourth instar the caterpillars were much larger; Pliable
and Timorous weighed 12/1000 ounce each, the former a little
more than the latter. The bands of darker color on the thorax and
hinder part of the body had now become distinct. The filaments
on the middle thorax were longer and darker, and the creatures
were moving toward the final strong patterning of the fully grown
caterpillar.

All this time, particularly in the third and fourth instars, the
caterpillars were exposed to attack by enemies. Timorous had been
shaken off a leaf to the ground, but sometimes he, Pliable, and
many other third- and fourth-instar caterpillars deliberately fell off
to escape from predators. Shortly after Timorous's fall a blue jay
in search of food fluttered onto the plant where Pliable was
feeding. She immediately fell to the ground and remained curled
up and perfectly still. The sight of many animals, and particularly
of birds, is more adapted to perceive motion than details of color

or shape. If she remained still the blue jay might not see her, and this indeed proved to be the case. But the same problem now faced her as had confronted Timorous—she had to find her way to a milkweed plant. This she could only do by random wandering; her senses of smell and sight were not strongly enough developed to locate her special food until she was actually in contact with a milkweed plant. Five minutes after her fall she started to move again. She crawled on a slightly wavy course until she almost touched a milkweed plant, but then she suddenly turned away from it at a right angle. All unknowing she had missed her chance. After five more minutes' progress, still on a wandering track, she came up against a young milkweed stem, recognized it as suitable, climbed up to a medium-sized leaf near the top, and started to feed at once. Food was badly needed, for she had used up a considerable amount in her wanderings. Falling from a milkweed plant and then being unable to find the way back onto another is a frequent cause of death among young larvae; this is one reason why caterpillars are more frequent among patches of milkweed than on scattered plants. It is also the reason isolated plants thrive better than do clumps; fewer of their leaves are eaten by monarchs.

Against disastrous falls caterpillars that feed on high trees have a protective device in the form of a silk line which is emitted from a special gland just below the mouth. The silk is attached to the leaf or twig on which the creature is feeding and as the insect falls more liquid silk is pumped out. The silk hardens on exposure to the air, and after falling a few feet the caterpillar stops issuing the substance, rests a little, and then climbs up its lifeline to return to its original spot, when it cuts the silk line away.

Monarch caterpillars, feeding on comparatively low plants, do not have much use for such lifelines but do have two comparatively

important uses for small quantities of silk. A thread can be spun
at times to help get a grip on a surface and to act as a guideline on
a leaf, so that a caterpillar could find its way back to a feeding
point, say an eggshell or a hole in a leaf; it is easier for a small
caterpillar to feed at a hole when the whole leaf can be bitten into,
than for it to have to rasp away and penetrate a surface. Feeding at
a hole is also easier than starting on the edge of a leaf; edges are
usually protected with thick palisade cells or even serrations. Silk is
also used at the time of pupation, as described later.

Pliable and Timorous made their silk in special glands situated
in the lower lip region, as do all caterpillars. The thick, sticky
liquid secreted there was squeezed through a small exit hole and
immediately hardened as it reached the air. It is in miniature much
the same process as that used for the production of artificial fibers,
such as nylon, where a sticky paste is forced through a small metal
nozzle and becomes a fine and strong thread on contact with air or
water. Silk is a protein and in nature protein foods are more
difficult to obtain than carbohydrates; the monarchs, which do not
climb to great heights as caterpillars, reserve their scarce protein
resources for other ends, mostly the building up of food reserves
for their active adult life.

Yet another molt (the fourth) awaited Pliable and Timorous
before pupation and their emergence as adult butterflies. This molt
must be considered in a little more detail; it was their last as
caterpillars. By August 26 Pliable had been feeding hungrily for
three days and had increased in weight from 12/1000 ounce to
about 25/1000; that is, she had more than doubled her weight in
a very short time, so that the pressure within her body was great
and becoming unpleasant. Since insects can grow only by making a
new skin beneath the old one and discarding the top one, it might
well be asked how they can grow to such an extent, for it would

seem that the new skin must be just that little bit smaller. The answer is that the new skin develops a number of folds which can expand like a concertina opening out when the old skin is discarded.

As the pressure within Pliable's body grew, it started an activity in some special cells of her brain which in turn acted on certain glands leading to the production of the molting hormone. Yet another gland, the *corpus allatum* ("causing body"), just behind the brain, was producing the juvenile hormone: both hormones entered her blood and insured that simple molting and not pupation took place. The hormones and the pressure within the body first induced a lethargic state. Pliable stopped eating, moved very slowly, and appeared to ignore her surroundings. Next she moved to a sheltered stop on the underside of a rather older milkweed leaf and remained motionless for two hours. Then she began slowly moving her four pairs of prolegs (the false legs on the abdomen, behind the three pairs of true legs on the thorax); by this means she secured a firm grasp of the leaf by insuring that the sucker contacts on each leg were well bedded down, for to fall off the leaf while molting would be fatal. The anal clasper (the hind pair of prolegs) she attached to the midrib of the leaf. Now safely anchored, she lowered the forward part of her body—the three thoracic segments and the head—and then curved her head upward. More of the molting hormone was then released into the blood, causing the cells on the inner side of the skin slowly to detach from the outer, tough, chitinized skin layer. The inner layer started to grow, producing the folds already mentioned. At the same time a "molting fluid" poured into the space between the two skins and dissolved the inner layers of the old cuticle; it did not dissolve the sclerotin, one of the ingredients of the outer skin. As the inner skin grew it absorbed the molting fluid; the space

16

between skins became almost dry, and only a thin but tough layer was left of the old skin. The separation of the two skins caused Pliable gradually to lose her bright colors from front to back as the process advanced. From time to time she gave a convulsive wriggle to assist in the separation. Finally she had to find a way of breaking out of what was left of the outer skin, a tough sclerotinized layer. Evolution over the millennia had provided a method; there are "molting sutures" in the skin, visible as white lines on the surface. These lines contained no sclerotin. Although normally quite strong they become weakened under the action of the molting fluid. Pliable built up her abdominal muscles and increased her blood pressure, which forced blood into her abdomen and thorax. She also absorbed some air, pumping that into the same region. After about an hour the pressure was too much for the old skin, which split along one of the sutures on the thorax. Wriggling and pumping her blood ever faster Pliable extended the split over her head, rested a minute, and then started to push her head out of the old skin, gradually drawing her body behind her until she was free. In addition to the body skin, Pliable also drew out the lining of the fore and hind gut, the whole being a most complex and difficult proceeding, full of dangers, both from predators and from accidents that could trap her between the old and new skins and leave her to die of exhaustion. Again she rested, relaxed the pressure, and moved away, but soon she returned and ate the old skin. There is great economy in the insect world. Sclerotin is a protein and proteins must not be wasted. Some female insects and some female spiders even eat their males after (or even during) copulation. Parental care being almost unknown in these species, the father contributes his share to the offspring by allowing his body to be used as food for the mother.

At this period Pliable was very sensitive to movement. The

vibrations from a truck passing on the nearby road induced an immediate defensive reaction, the raising of her black head to show both that and the brown and yellow markings of her fifth-instar skin, together with the twitching of the filaments on the thorax and rear segment.

In all Pliable took about five hours to complete the molt; Timorous, always slower, needed double the time, but he too successfully completed it on August 29. They were now in their final caterpillar stage and wore a striking livery of heavy black stripes on a yellow ground, but the pattern was not exactly standard for all caterpillars of the species. Pliable, for instance, had narrower and slightly lighter black bands than Timorous and the latter's yellow was more creamy. The filaments on the thorax were now long and very black and another pair of filaments had developed on the rear segment of the body. After their rest, Pliable, Timorous, and many other members of their species set about the next and most serious stage of their lives—eating enormously. Pliable now weighed 50/1000 ounce and Timorous a little less. Both were soon hard at work eating the milkweed leaves, traveling to a new leaf as soon as one was consumed. As they moved they waved their long feelers to draw attention to themselves, as if to say "Look at my lovely colors" but in reality as one of their defense mechanisms.

A fourth- or fifth-instar caterpillar is a good meal for a bird, particularly for one with a nest of hungry chicks to feed. Many birds, such as the scavenging sparrows, will feed their young only on animal food, a considerable proportion of this being insects. Some caterpillars try to avoid that danger by camouflage; being much the same color as their food, mostly different shades of green, they may remain invisible. The larva of the common wood nymph (*Satyrus alope*) is long, thin, and green; it feeds on grasses and is difficult to see when clinging to a stem. Although the adults vary in their markings according to their region (Long Island to Florida), the caterpillars are all very similar. Other caterpillars may mimic some natural feature, such as a twig. The brownish caterpillar of the peppered moth (*Biston betularius*) when at rest clings to a twig with its anal clasper and stands stiff and erect, exactly resembling a piece of the tree on whose foliage it is feeding. The creature even has a fringe of little protuberances to cover the join between the insect and the twig it is grasping, in order to make this join less noticeable. Still others rely on defensive and threatening movements, such as those used by the young monarch caterpillars, which raise their heads and sway from side to side and on other occasions remain perfectly still and sham dead. A defense mechanism among adult butterflies is the sudden exposure of ocelli, or eye spots, similar to the "eyes" on peacock feathers; this device is also found in caterpillars. The swallowtail butterfly (*Papilio troilus*) has on its hind segment a pair of horns, which it can project, erect, and wave, and also two large eye spots which can suddenly be produced—one presumes for the purpose of frightening enemies away. The hind parts of this caterpillar at such a moment look very much like the head of a snake, but a very small one. Why an enemy, say a bird, should be frightened by a tiny facsimile of a snake remains an enigma.[3]

Pliable, Timorous, and the rest of their generation used a number of these defense devices, as well as an important one not yet mentioned—a disagreeable taste. Their digestive systems enabled them to extract the poisonous, bad-tasting chemicals in the milkweed plant and store them in their bodies with no harmful effects on themselves. Predacious birds soon learn that the monarch caterpillars are not good eating and leave them alone; the lesson is reinforced by the striking colors and waving tentacles, all in effect saying, "Here I am; eat me if you dare; I'll make you sick." In addition to these warning colors, monarchs in moments of danger excrete a warning smell which further reinforces the message.

While in the early instars the caterpillars fall to the ground to escape enemies, in the fifth instar their tentacles are long enough to be waved about and either frighten or wipe off any creature, such as an ichneumon wasp, that is trying to lay eggs in the caterpillar's body.

Pliable was much worried by a small bristly fly feeding on the pale red milkweed flowers; instinctively she knew it was dangerous. The creature was an *Exorista* and belonged to a family of Tachinid flies noted for being parasitic on other insects; they are thus useful to man when members of the family attack crop pests, such as the cotton worm. This particular *Exorista* was a female, full of fertile eggs and longing to lay them in the right spot. She would try to settle on a nice fat caterpillar and quickly lay a sticky egg. Not only would the sticky material fix the egg fast to the caterpillar, but the egg, once laid, would rapidly hatch and the young fly grub bore at once into the caterpillar's body. There it would feed extremely carefully, to avoid killing its host prematurely. The grub would consume the less important muscle and the protein and fat stores in the caterpillar's body, and only when ready to pupate would it attack a vital part, such as the heart or central nerve system, and kill the host. The grubs would then bore out of the caterpillar, and emerge as adult flies ready to start the cycle again.

The *Exorista* made repeated attempts to settle on Pliable, which fortunately the caterpillar was always able to prevent. She waved her tentacles across her body, gave sudden jerks and twists, and finally got rid of her attacker by the most dangerous of her defense mechanisms—falling to the ground. To the *Exorista* her prey seemed to have vanished into thin air, for on falling Pliable curled up and remained perfectly still and thus was not noticed by the fly. The *Exorista* buzzed around the milkweed for a little, then abandoned the search and flew some ten yards away, still diligently searching for caterpillars of suitable size in which to lay her eggs. Pliable had to repeat this performance on many occasions, sometimes having to resort to the ultimate defense of falling, sometimes frightening her tiny enemy away with flailings and jerkings of her body. All this was a great disadvantage to her, for at each attack she lost valuable time which should have been devoted to feeding.

Timorous was also exposed to similar attack by a different insect, an ichneumon wasp, a species of *Temelucha*. Timorous had an easier task than Pliable, for as it happened he was only attacked by *Temelucha*. The parasite had to get into just the right position to strike and Timorous could swing his tentacles over his body to wipe the attacker off in much the same way that a horse removes flies with a swish of its tail. Because of the tentacles, not many monarch caterpillars are parasitized by ichneumons, though there sometimes are exceptional seasons. Both Pliable and Timorous continued to eat, eat, and eat. They preferred the young leaves, but these were scarce in a dry late August, and they often had to turn to the tougher, older leaves. This had the effect of increasing the amount of poison in their bodies, which was not an advantage to them personally, since by the time a bird discovered how bad they tasted they would already have been bitten and would die. Once the outer skin is even moderately punctured, the pressure maintaining the insect's shape and very being is lost; the creature collapses like a flat tire. In the insect world the individual is not of much importance. The accumulation of the milkweed poisons benefited the race. Birds got to know that large monarch caterpillars were even more horrible than small ones. The experience tended to be passed on to their descendants and might eventually become instinctive.

Sometimes Timorous would eat through the midrib of a leaf and cause it to bend over, giving him a little extra shade and shelter from enemies. On the whole, both he and Pliable ate holes in the leaves, leaving the main veins alone; sometimes these holes had an untouched vein passing through the eaten away patch. They were reaching their maximum size and weighed about 56/1000 ounce each. To reach this weight Pliable had eaten 1 ½ ounces of milkweed leaves and Timorous, slightly smaller, had taken a little less. Small as these figures seem, Pliable had consumed 25 times her own weight in food. A human being between birth and eighteen years of age eats about 7 tons of food—that is, some 1,750 times his or her own weight. The monarch's main food consumption, however, is made over a mere 14 to 20 days. It is a full-time job and interruptions, such as are caused by warding off predators, falling off a plant, or bad weather, are a serious setback to growth.

Pliable and Timorous had increased in weight from about 2/100,000 ounce at birth to about 55/1000 ounce, an increase of 2,750 times. In comparison, the increase of a human from birth to full growth—8 pounds to 160 pounds, say, is a mere 20 times. Such comparisons are frequently made, but they are not quite legitimate. The human offspring starts with the fusion of male and female cells to make a zygote, which is about the same weight as that of the monarch butterfly. This zygote grows to a 160-pound individual, or thereabouts, an increase of several million times; the human is well ahead in the ultimate weight-increase stakes. The remarkable thing about the butterfly is it gets its nearly 3,000-fold increase in less than three weeks, while the human needs about 18 years.

Also, 1 ½ ounces per butterfly does not sound like much food, but as the butterflies occur in millions the total eaten is considerable. Pliable and Timorous were but two of some 10 million monarchs in the eastern United States that year, and these creatures had thus eaten about 470 tons of milkweed, a considerable quantity of a rather scattered plant.

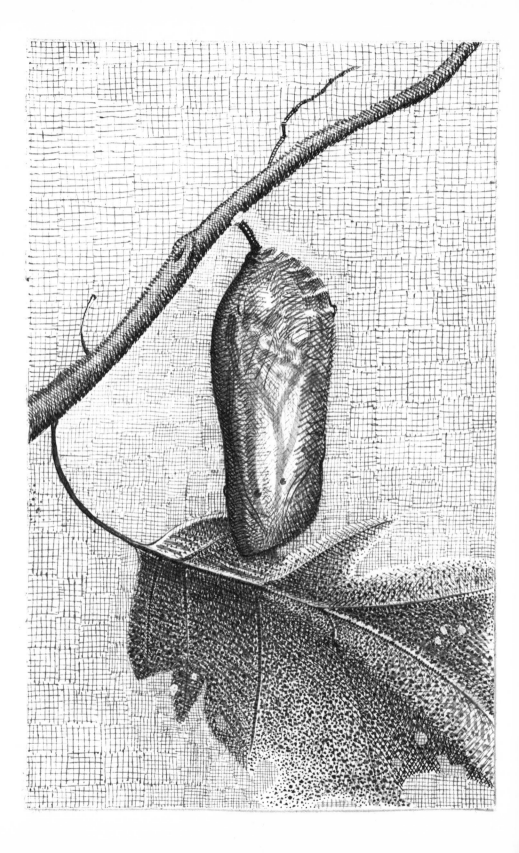

2 THE CHRYSALIS STAGE

AUGUST 29 – SEPTEMBER 14

Pupation, the next great crisis in the lives of Pliable and Timorous, was now rapidly approaching. The lives of insects are in fact a series of physical crises—molts, pupation, and emergence as an adult; at any of these points the slightest slip can lead to death. In addition to the risks of the actual pupation process itself, Timorous and Pliable, and all their kind, were constantly exposed to the attacks of predators, parasites, and diseases. Theirs was a natural existence.

In the last days of August Pliable ate furiously; it was her last opportunity to obtain the protein reserves needed for the rest of her life. The reaction to the pressure building up in her body by intensive feeding was to induce the glands in her head once more to produce the molting hormone, but as she had aged the amount of the corresponding juvenile hormone from the *corpus allatum* was reduced. This had the effect of inducing pupation rather than a simple molt. By August 29 the quantities of the two hormones were just balanced enough to set the pupation reaction in train.

She stopped feeding, hurriedly left the milkweed plant by falling to the ground, expelled excreta, and rapidly crawled away. The urgency of her movements was due to the fact that the pupa was forming within her skin and before the reaction prohibited movement she had to find a safe place in which this change could take place. The site she wanted had to be protected more from physical dangers than enemies, particularly from the wind's blowing stems against her while the soft pupa was forming. Any interference could cause her to emerge as a deformed adult, if it did not kill her. After wandering for 10 feet she climbed 2 feet up an old fallen branch and hung head down from a cross twig, waving her body around in a circle to see if there was anything nearby likely to strike her in a wind. Her head came into contact with a grass stem and she immediately abandoned the site, setting off on her quest once more. She came across a bunch of milkweed stems and immediately turned away from them. Those plants once so essential to her now seemed to repel. Hurriedly she moved on and examined three other sites before she found an old post-and-rail fence running east and west. She had been searching for two hours.

Pliable climbed to the first rail of the fence and moved eastward about 2 inches along the underside of the rail. Here she was protected from the west wind. Hanging downward she slowly rotated her body, testing the position for obstacles, and after an hour's work she appeared to be satisfied that there were none. Next she started to spin silk from the orifice on her lower lip, waving her head slowly and deliberately backward and forward over a patch on the underside of the rail. The sticky silk caught on the rough wood and a mat of coarse silk fibers started to form there. She built in more fibers at the center and made a dense round button of silk, doing the work slowly and resting from time to time. She then rested an hour and then, twisting around, she grasped the silk button with her anal clasper, working it back and forth until the curved hooks on it were firmly entangled with the silk She then lowered her body and twisted the fore part upward to form a U shape. She tested this position once or twice and then lowered the free arm of the U a little, lengthening the attached arm until the shape was more that of a capital J. At the same time a color change was taking place. The bright yellow and orange bands became duller and turned blue, an indication that the pupa had now formed within the caterpillar skin.

Pliable now started to pump blood into her thorax, which, swelling, caused the old skin to split just behind her head. She now had to perform some extraordinary acrobatics—while hanging head downward above an apparently bottomless void, to let go of her only support and catch on again somewhere else. By means of her wriggling, contracting, and expanding, the old skin was gradually pushed upward toward the rear end and the mat of silk fibers. The anal clasper which supported her was covered with the old skin. If all the old skin was discarded the pupa forming within the skin would fall to the ground, which would be absolutely fatal to the creature. To avoid this, Pliable, like all her kind, had a special organ, the cremaster, a hard chitinized knob at the end of the pupa. The word is derived from the Greek and means "to suspend." Pliable withdrew her cremaster from the old skin, allowed the knob, which was provided with a number of chitinized hooks, to harden, and then pushed it up into the silk mat. She next started to turn round and round. This action firmly embedded the cremaster hooks in the silk and caused the old skin to drop away and fall to the ground. She was now a soft blue pupa, in a condition known as semi-exarate (from the furrowlike lines on the surface; the word comes from the Latin *exare,* to plow) and on her way to becoming a hard, fully formed chrysalis. As a semi-exarate she was particularly vulnerable. She could have been damaged not only by external objects falling upon her or rubbing against her but even by the rough spines and projections of the old skin itself as she struggled free of it.

Not all butterflies and moths pupate in the same way or for the same length of time. There are three main methods:

First: The pupa hangs down, head downward, with no other support than the tail and attachment, as described for the monarch. This system is used by the Danaidae (the monarchs) and most of the Satyridae (the ringlets, wood nymphs, browns, and others).

Second: The pupa is attached by the tail but also supported by a silken girdle tending to raise the head, as in the Papilionidae and Pieridae.

Third: The pupa is enclosed in a cocoon, as in the case of the silkworm.

The first method and its difficulties have been described. In the second method, the old skin has to be removed and, in addition to being freed from the silk mat after the cremaster has been bedded into it, must also be passed under the silk girdle supporting the pupa against a stem, a matter of no little difficulty.

In the third method the pupa has a cocoon over it: spinning this is a complicated process and uses up a considerable quantity of the caterpillar's food reserves. The cocoon also makes the emergence of the adult insect more difficult. The whole process of pupation is, in fact, fraught with difficulties; this is one of the reasons that insects are not the dominant life form on earth. Another reason is the exoskeleton; vertebrates are much more efficient.

Timorous went through the same processes on September 1, three days later than Pliable. He selected the underside of a dead

28

branch as his pupation site, after having tested and rejected several others. He was particularly wary of leaves at this late stage of the season. Perhaps the maturity or rigidity of the leaves seemed to warn him that they were dangerous. Though the underside of a leaf seems to be a good site, being sheltered and inconspicuous, if the leaf falls it will take the pupa with it. On the ground the adult would not be able to emerge properly and if it emerges at all will almost certainly be deformed. The pupa also might be eaten by shrews, which were always scuttling about looking for food. The dead branch finally satisfied Timorous. He was 100 yards away from Pliable, on the other side of the milkweed patch.

He had some difficulty in rejecting his old caterpillar skin. A scouting ant kept coming around, but by jerking his body and oozing his ant-repellent Timorous managed to drive the creature off and at the same time free himself from his old integument.

In the semi-exarate state, Pliable and Timorous looked more like fat grubs than like caterpillars or pupae. They were a little more than 1 inch long and ½ inch in diameter at the widest part. They weighed about 1/20 ounce each. The three body segments were marked by deep furrows. The wing buds could be seen and now started to expand, their growth being no longer inhibited by the presence of the juvenile hormone. Various other parts also could be seen on the soft new pupae—head, legs, and particularly new mouth parts. The change in the mouth is as striking a difference between caterpillar and butterfly as is the appearance of wings. Parts of the caterpillar's biting jaws, the galeae, elongate, become semicircular, with rigid flanges, and are fitted together to form a sucking tube—the proboscis of the butterfly. These could be seen forming on the surface of the pupae.

Pliable and Timorous gradually began to lose their grublike appearance. The furrows filled out, the skin hardened, becoming bluish-green in color, and a number of shiny gold spots appeared. They were now fully formed chrysalises. The process had taken Pliable a day; once again Timorous was a little slower. Both chrysalises had a number of shiny golden spots on them. The word chrysalis comes from the Greek word meaning "gold"; the name was given by early naturalists because of the golden markings and golden color of so many of those structures.

These glowing points were a notable feature of Pliable in her chrysalis form. As the chrysalis turned to blue-green, the white, silvery band around her uppermost part that bore the gold spots became shiny black. Other gold spots were scattered over the surface, always in the same places in all monarch pupae. Unlike that of the caterpillar and adult butterfly, the pupa's coloring is muted, as though designed to escape detection. The pupa is hard and probably distasteful to birds, but it seems to rely for safety chiefly on concealment. The spots make the pupa, which is about an inch long, look like a piece of modern jewelry—an expensive earring in jade and gold. Live fireflies and butterflies were at one time used as hair decorations by the ladies of Brazil; perhaps a pair of earrings made from hatching monarch pupae would create a sensation at a fashionable party. But the situation would be fraught with difficulty both for the poor creatures themselves and for the lady wearing them. They would flutter and tickle under her ears as they hatched, and might hatch before the guests arrived.

Since the spots are not there to break the pattern (they are too small) or to assist concealment, it may well be asked what biological end they serve. This is to assume that every characteristic an animal has is "useful," a point that is discussed later in connection with the adult monarchs. As for the gold spots, Dr. F. A. Urquhart, the Canadian entomologist who is a leading authority on the monarch, once named all these and dissected out some of them; beneath such a spot he found a series of bright, diamondlike scales which reflected the light back through the yellow pigment. Urquhart thought that in all probability these spots were light receptors.[1] To emerge successfully from the pupa, the monarch needs to appear in sunlight and calm weather, and these spots may be its substitute for the photographer's photoelectric light meter. On a dull day the spots, in effect, send a message to the monarch brain inside the pupa: "Delay emergence; light is only 14 lux." In sunny calm weather they say: "Now's the time; get cracking." Literally cracking, for the pupa is split open by pressure from within in the same way as the old skin of the caterpillar is cracked off when the new one is formed within it. Very few butterflies emerge in dull weather or at night, so obviously there is a mechanism in the pupa regulating this.

Numerous changes take place within the pupa before the adult emerges and many of these changes can be seen from the outside of the fully formed pupa. Having been semi-exarate, Pliable was now "obtect." That is, her appendages were no longer free, as when the pupa was first formed, but were gummed down to the external pupal case, showing a semitransparent, hard, smooth, waxy, light-blue skin to the world. This change took a day.

That Pliable had a ring structure could clearly be seen from the pupa: the rings were very obvious, particularly in the abdominal region, which was the upper end of the pupa, where the cremaster attached her to the fence rail, but was the hinder part of her body as she hung head downward. On her underside two pairs of legs could be seen—the first and second pairs. The first pair was small and she would hardly use them at all as an adult. The second pair was well marked, but the third pair could not be observed from the outside, being concealed by the mouthparts and other organs. Of course, she had to breathe, and the series of spiracles through which air diffused still existed and were used continuously.

On the undersides of the pupae other features besides the legs could be distinguished. These were the antennae, much more important to the adult than to the caterpillar and now showing quite large, and two huge compound eyes which were now developed and replacing the simple eyes of the larvae. As caterpillars Timorous and Pliable could not see very much: in spite of having six eyes each, they could just about distinguish light from dark and they found their food by a contact sense. The eyes just served enough to say, in effect, "It's daylight; start feeding again." The skin was also light-sensitive. When the two caterpillars touched the right food they knew it and remained in touch with it as long as they could. Sight and smell played very little part as a guide to their feeding as caterpillars; by contrast, as adults these would be the most important senses.

On the pupae the wings were also beginning to show. Each adult would have two pairs, but only the forewings could be seen with any ease in the pupa; on careful examination a small strip of hindwing was visible. On the thoracic region each pupa had a pair of breathing spiracles and there was also a pair on each of the first eight of the ten abdominal rings.

Timorous, about 100 yards away, pupated at about the same time that Pliable did. The only difference between the pupae was that Pliable's sexual orifice was on the eighth abdominal ring, whereas that of Timorous was on the ninth.

Another important change was taking place within the pupae. As caterpillars Pliable and Timorous were continually eating foliage. They had large stomachs—a food reservoir—and as the food contained much indigestible fiber they had a big excretory system. There were a lot of feces to get rid of, as anyone who has kept caterpillars will know. Within the pupa the esophagus, or throat, became lengthened and the stomach much reduced, for as adults they would only take liquids. Although the pupa takes no food—in this respect it is like a second egg stage—metabolism continues. Pliable and Timorous breathed and used up some of their food reserves, so that they too had waste products to get rid of—the meconium. These accumulated in a special little sac in the abdomen. Water is a very precious product for a pupa. Since it neither feeds nor drinks, the pupa cannot afford to waste this vital substance. Special organs in the abdomen, the Malpighian tubes, extract waste products from the blood, passing them to the hind gut chambers where water is extracted and reused—a process comparable to the "recycling" of waste products in industry. The excreta accumulate as a dark-colored thin paste. Since the cuticle of the pupa is impervious to water there are no direct evaporation losses from the skin. Dew soaking into the spiracles adds a little water to the system from time to time, and valves in these same spiracles prevent water from leaving it. As conservers of water and economizers in its use, Pliable and Timorous were well in advance of the camel.

While their various organs were developing the pupae changed color. On August 29 Pliable was a shade of blue-green. The color darkened slowly and by September 8 she was a dark gray, gradually darkening to brown on September 10. By the next day the reddish-orange color of the wings was visible and one day later (September 12) the wings could be seen clearly. Pliable began to give slight convulsions and twists, indications that the moment for emergence as an adult was at hand. Timorous reached the same stage on September 14.

3 OUT INTO THE WORLD

SEPTEMBER 12 – 17

The importance of passing from infancy to adulthood is recognized by most animals. Caterpillars store up immense reserves of food in their bodies, choose pupation sites very carefully, and, as emerging adults, dress in most elaborate patterns. In the human species, the aspirants, particularly the males, prove their worth by elaborate initiation ceremonies, such as mock or real battles in the so-called primitive tribes and sporting contests in the more affluent nations. People in nearly all walks of life celebrate with parties when a child becomes adult. While butterflies do not do this, it could be argued that they make an equally important gesture. Though the caterpillar eats its eggshell on birth, the butterfly does not eat the old pupal skin but discards it for the ants. This is valuable protein and represents as big a percentage of the insect's wealth as an Indian initiation ceremony, a bar mitzvah, or an eighteenth or twenty-first birthday party does for a human parent, bigger in fact. This action, of course, is not

35

due to generosity on the part of the butterfly, but to the fact that the creature has not yet found any way to make use of the material.

Pliable was ready to emerge as an adult on September 12, and her senses told her that conditions were right—the sun shone and there was no wind. The convulsions along the pupa continued. There were a number of weak fracture lines in the pupal skin and the first one cracked at 10:30 a.m.; it was in the center of a small plate covering the head and thus at the bottom of the hanging pupa. Pliable's first bid for freedom was soon followed by another thrust which split the skin along the upper side of her thorax. She then rested for half a minute before renewing her efforts. The plate over her head broke away and curled back; the skin over the lower side of the thorax split along two lines from front to back and only remained attached to the pupa at the rear (upper) end. She was making good progress, which so far had taken 1½ minutes.

After resting a moment Pliable thrust one of her middle legs through the split on her stomach side and vainly waved it around in an effort to make contact with a solid object to give herself leverage for the rest of the operation and to prevent herself from falling to the ground. Since she had been careful to select a pupation site free from possible interference, her present search for a nearby support was not likely to be successful, but such help was not needed. Ten seconds later she put out the second leg of the middle pair and then split the cap off over her head. A final fracture along the circle of gold spots now allowed her to withdraw from the pupa. She extracted all six legs, though she only used four of them, and grasped the pupal case. She pulled out her thorax and then her abdomen, which seemed very long, plump, and reminiscent of the caterpillar. Next she drew out two pairs of small, fleshy, black-and-orange wings and hung limply clinging to the old case with what seemed to be two pairs of extraordinarily long legs. She then turned around so that her head was uppermost and the wings hung down. This position would facilitate the important operation of pumping up the wings.

Pliable had taken only three minutes to reach this stage. Butterflies are most vulnerable to enemies at this point and the operation has to be conducted as quickly as possible. Ants are a threat; they continually send out scouts looking for food, especially high-protein food such as a well-fed butterfly. Pliable, like all her kind, met this threat by promptly secreting a repellent substance.

Pliable's middle and hind pairs of legs appeared to be long because they were still soft and were stuck straight out, instead of being bent at various joints as in the normal position. Her front pair of legs were held up tight against her thorax and were hardly used. Her long mouth was curled into a spiral under her head. Her two enormous eyes glistened in the sunlight. The long and delicate antennae quickly dried; at first they lay along her back but soon she was moving them, gaining much information as to the shape, size, position, smell, and sound of the new world she was to inhabit. She was still extremely vulnerable, and her next task was to perfect her wings.

A butterfly wing consists of two chitinous membranes, an upper and a lower, with an air space between them. The membranes are strengthened by "nerves"—a series of branching tubes making a distinctive pattern for each species. These patterns are used by entomologists to classify the creatures. The term nerves is not a good one, as the organs in question are no part of the nervous system and neither transmit nor receive messages to or from the brain. Either "nervules" or "wing skeleton" would be better names for these tubes. The chitin does not stretch and the wings as they emerge from the pupal case have a number of folds or corrugations in them, which allow them to expand, as do the folds in the new skin of a caterpillar.

The wings of the monarchs are covered with tiny scales which provide their colors and patterns in two ways. The scales are tinted with pigments pumped into them in the last few days of pupal life, and some are covered with little lines (striae) that break up light falling on them and give different iridescent colors according to the angle at which they are seen.

Scales are a remarkable feature of the wings of butterflies and moths. These insects are in the order Lepidoptera, a name signifying "scaly wing." The scales are of various shapes and sizes and overlap one another in the manner of tiles on a roof. They are, in fact, modified hairs and have intrigued naturalists ever since the magnifying glass was developed and probably before. Thomas Mouffet (or Muffet), a fashionable London doctor of Elizabethan times who wrote a book on insects in Latin that contained some of the earliest accurate descriptions of butterflies, noted the dust from their wings and compared the wings to feathers.[1] The great eighteenth-century French *Encyclopédie* contains a very good description of the creatures; the writer resented the wing scales' being likened to feathers: "These small plates have very incorrectly been given the name of feathers because they are found on the wings: the word *scales* would be more suitable." [2] The article is unsigned but in all probability was written by the French naturalist René de Réaumur and includes many accurate observations.

The remains of Pliable's pupal case were still attached to the silk button on the fencing rail and Pliable hung on to the case for dear life; a fall would have damaged her still soft wings and have exposed her to attacks from shrews, mice, and possibly ants. With her head upward her wings hung down. She started to pump blood from her abdomen into the wings, pumping for a few seconds and then resting for slightly longer. The wings, marked in a pattern of brilliant orange-brown and velvety black, slowly started to expand. The two skins of the wings do not swell out as a child's balloon does when blown up, as they have a number of joining links within them holding the two surfaces close together.

Every now and then Pliable practiced unrolling her long tongue and then coiling it up again. Next she slowly opened and closed her wings and appeared to be more satisfied with them on each occasion. The sunlight and warm air were gradually hardening them. As the fluid in her abdomen was transferred to the wings the abdomen contracted to a more normal butterfly size. From time to time she flexed a leg and then voided a drop of the excreta that had been accumulating during pupation.

In past ages the passing of this fluid sometimes gave rise to considerable alarm. It frequently is red and the drops are sometimes voided when the butterfly is first flying. As is well known, butterflies can occur in considerable numbers. Consequently if the drops are red and the creatures are numerous, the effect is one of a shower of blood, enough to frighten any community until it is explained rationally. Frank Cowan, the late-nineteenth-century Philadelphia entomologist, accumulated much information on these alarms, beginning with accounts by Livy in classical Roman times and continuing with many later records. In Frankfurt in 1296 such a shower threw suspicion on the Jews and led to a massacre of some 10,000 of them. The first rational explanation of these "bloody rains" was given by a Monsieur Peirese, in July 1608, at Aix in France. This gentleman had noticed that a pupa he had kept in a box had hatched into a beautiful butterfly and had left a red stain "as big as a sou" in the box. It was probably a small tortoiseshell (*Vanessa urticae*) ; the species was very numerous that year. Peirese

39

argued that if each butterfly left a red drop on emergence this could be the cause of the red rain, not the work of the devil or of witches who killed innocent young children for the purpose. He examined sites where the "blood" was found and others where it did not occur. The stains were not on rooftops, where they would have been had the blood fallen from the sky, but were on walls and in sheltered places where butterflies could have rested after emergence from the pupae. He gathered a body of people together and showed them the sites, but one feels that many of his auditors would not have given up the mystical explanation, or at least have given it up with reluctance, in favor of the rational. Still, perhaps he saved the lives of some poor old women.[3]

Pliable continued to practice moving her coiled mouth and her wings. The formation of sucking mouth parts from biting jaws during the pupal stage is one of the most remarkable things in natural history. The galeae of the maxillae (jaws), which form the proboscis, became enormously developed; that organ now consisted of two lateral halves united down the middle to form three tubes. Each half consisted of a large number of short transverse rings, convex on the outer surface and concave on the inner. When these two halves were pressed together the large central tube was formed, the halves being held together by a series of interlocking hooks, rather like a zipper. The large tube connected with a food reservoir, and liquids could be sucked up this tube by the action of a sac in the head. Two smaller tubes, or tracheae, within the two maxillae were used to excrete saliva.

When Pliable extended her mouth it was as long as her body; retracted, it had about four coils. The whole device was worked by powerful lateral muscles, and about a third of the way along the tube (counting from the head) were some special muscles which resisted the uncoiling of the tube. The effect was to make a "knee joint" at this point; the mouth did not stick straight out from her head but had a bend of about 120 degrees, enabling her more easily to insert it into flowers and suck up the nectar so vital to her survival and journeyings. Another characteristic of this remarkable mouth is that when coiled it is flattish, like a thick piece of ribbon, and when extended it is a tube. An analogy is the steel measuring tape which is coiled flat in its box when at rest and of curved section when pulled out straight for use; the curvature gives the tape its rigidity. Pliable's mouth was like two such tapes joined, with leakproof edges, each curved almost to a semicircle.

At this stage Pliable was instinctively aware of two things: she was in danger until capable of controlled flight, and she was hungry and must continue to accumulate food reserves for the coming winter. She had a time/danger problem to solve. If she took off too soon her flight would be weak and at the mercy of gusty winds and possibly of some birds, but every minute she waited she was exposed to dangers from ants and other animals. She had chosen a good day for emergence, sunny, warm, and without wind. Her wings had quickly hardened. Suddenly she took flight; there was no preparatory wing movement. She was a splendid sight. The upper surfaces of the wings were bright reddish-brown with black borders to the fore and hind wings, the borders having white spots. Black veins ran through the center portions of the wings. A few brown rings circled the body which also had some white spots. She was large for a butterfly. Her wingspread was 4 inches, and a few rapid beats of the two pairs raised her 6 feet into the air, flashing and darting in the sunlight. She turned and made a zigzag line for the milkweed patch where the late flowers were still opening.

The entomology student was seated in this patch and caught

her with one stroke of a butterfly net. For Pliable it was a shattering experience: aeons of natural selection had not prepared her for anything like this, especially so soon after emergence.

The two young people with their "laboratory" at the gas station had decided earlier to catch monarchs, mark them, and release them, in the hope that some would be caught and the captures reported. Much has been learned about bird migration by putting rings on young birds; a surprising number of these have been found again. The recapture of a marked butterfly is more difficult. Butterflies do not live as long as birds, and dead butterflies are soon eaten by shrews or ants. As they can only be marked by small plastic or paper labels, these are easily lost. The gas station made a feature of the monarchs, changing its name to "Butterfly Gas" and distributing leaflets showing a labeled butterfly, particularly to customers from the south. It also sold butterfly nets as a sideline.

To carry out this program, the young people had to capture monarchs and breed them in large numbers. The labeling presents physical difficulties; after many experiments, starting as early as 1796, entomologists have found that the best method is to use the kind of latex labels employed for price tags in stores, folding these over a patch on the forewing from which the scales have been scraped. This was the method used at the Glens Falls gas station. Each label had a number on one side and on the other side read: "Return to Box XYZ, Glens Falls, N.Y. 12801."

After capturing Pliable the student put her in a small cage containing some milkweed flowers and a piece of sponge soaked in a honey-and-water mixture. Pliable soon recovered from her shock and turned to sucking up honey from the sponge. Then she felt the urge to fly and began fluttering against the screen. Suddenly night came on, with no twilight at all, and Pliable settled down to rest, clinging to a twig; the cage had been put into a closet in the "laboratory."

On the far side of the milkweed patch were some poplar and willow trees, where a number of caterpillars of a different species of butterfly had been feeding. They were viceroys (*Basilarchia dissipus*). Two caterpillars, a male and a female, which I will call "Two-tongues" and "Lady Feigning," again from *Pilgrim's Progress*, had pupated on the twigs of an old apple tree and emerged as adults on September 12, the same day that Pliable did. The adult butterflies had a close resemblance to monarchs; this is the origin of the name viceroy, suggesting that they can take the place of the monarch. In point of fact, they cannot, for they belong to a different family, live on different food, and have a very different life history. The two species cannot mate together, and the caterpillars of the two kinds are quite different. Two-tongues and Lady Feigning had been caterpillars of the second-generation viceroys, in color dirty-white with a grayish underside and brown and bluish spots, and having two knobby appendages each.

Viceroys have two generations a year. The first arises from the overwintering caterpillars, which become adult about May. These give rise to the second generation, becoming adult in the early fall. Two-tongues and Lady Feigning belonged to this generation. After feeding avidly, as all caterpillars do, they had found pupation sites on an old apple tree and had emerged as adults on September 12.

The similarity of monarch and viceroy adults is remarkable. Lady Feigning's wing colors were also reddish-brown with a black border spotted with white. The general patterns was similar too, though her black veins were rather more strongly marked than were

43

Pliable's and the white spots on the forewings were fewer. Lady Feigning was smaller than Pliable, with a wingspan of 2 ¾ inches as compared to Pliable's 4 inches.

In spite of being so similar in appearance, viceroys and monarchs take very little notice of each other. The question arises: why are they so much alike? Is it pure coincidence, or does the similarity have some advantage for one or the other or both?

About 1859 an English naturalist, H. W. Bates (1825–1892), while collecting butterflies in Brazil, developed a theory on the subject. It was that some insects, particularly butterflies such as the monarch, developed a taste unpleasant to birds, either by extracting poisons from the plants on which they fed or by actually manufacturing unsavory substances in their bodies. Birds learned not to attack them. Then other butterflies started to develop patterns similar to those of the bad-tasting butterflies and as a result were also left alone.[4] This phenomenon was known as "Batesian mimicry." A little later the entomologist Fritz Müller of Brazil suggested that certain kinds of related insects, all unpalatable in varying degrees, come to resemble one another. Each species will then lose fewer individuals when the predators are in the learning stage. This is known as "Müllerian mimicry." The Encyclopaedia Britannica compares Batesian mimicry to "an unscrupulous merchant who copies the advertisement of a successful firm"; Müllerian mimicry to "a union of firms to adopt a common advertisement and share the expenses, the expense in the case of the insects being the loss of some individuals while the predators are learning of their unpalatable nature."[5]

One principal objection to the two theories was that good-tasting mimics were sometimes more numerous than the bad-tasting model, which would mean that a predator going for that particular pattern would more often have a tasty morsel than a disagreeable experience. Critics also pointed out that in many species only females mimicked and that birds in any case do not attack butterflies to a very great extent. Today, however, mimicry is thought to have some survival value, particularly in the tropics.[6]

Within any species different strains or races may appear and this is now thought to be the case with monarchs. Other differences are also seen, such as those in the wing patterns.[7] Recently a difference between the taste of different monarch butterflies of the same species has been discovered by Professor L. P. Brower of Amherst College. He found that some monarchs are much more repugnant to blue jays than others, and those that are distasteful and poisonous are so violently so that the birds which take them vomit almost at once and thereafter leave the species alone for life. The highly poisonous monarchs are sufficiently numerous to give the species a general protection.[8] It can be assumed that this characteristic has come to the fore fairly recently in bird, or butterfly, or both, for it is not yet instinctive. The birds have to learn by practical experience that some monarchs, usually about two-thirds of them, are unpleasant to eat.

An exciting study of patterns and mimicry has been made by Roger Caillois. He thinks that certain attributes of man, such as disguise, the use of masks, and the making of patterns, can be found in insects and other animals, but whereas these are external in man, animals have to adapt their physiology to create them. He says:

"Everything seems to happen as if they were following a *fashion*, to which each species adapts its livery by the means at its disposal: it is a slow-moving fashion, one where the changes take thousands of years, not a season, and which is concerned with whole species and not with individuals." [9]

At this stage, Pliable was not concerned with sex, but Lady Feigning was in a hurry. She had to lay fertile eggs very soon, for the caterpillars that would hatch from them had to have time to develop to the stage where they could form their winter shelter, the hibernaculum. In its second instar the second-generation viceroy caterpillar feeds in such a way that the leaf curls to form a tunnel. In order to set this process in motion, Lady Feigning first had to find a mate.

Timorous had emerged as an adult two days later than Pliable and the two viceroys. His markings were similar to Pliable's, but the black marginal band was slightly narrower, and on the first median nerve of the hind wing was a black scent pouch. Males are readily recognized by this black spot on the hind wing. He was soon flying, testing the strength of his wings and feeding on the delicious nectar of the milkweed, blackberry, and goldenrod flowers. His testes were developing and he began to feel an urge somewhere between play and sexual attraction, which was manifested by chasing after moving objects. He would wait on a leaf, keeping a careful watch for any of his comrades flying by. That his interest was not entirely sexually motivated was indicated by the fact that he was stimulated into a semisexual reaction by all sorts of movement. His first adventure of this kind, on September 15, was to set off after a torn scrap of newspaper caught up by a swirl of wind. The bit of paper behaved in such an unlepidopterous way, simply falling to earth, drifting along the ground, and jamming against the stem of a bush, that Timorous soon abandoned that chase. His very large, good eyes could easily distinguish a piece of paper from a butterfly, or even a monarch from other species, but the rising sexual urge and the movement of objects through the air created an atmosphere of excitement which nullified the evidence of his eyes. This "blindness" was manifested several times that day. He set off after a small bird and soon lost that. Once or twice he went down after falling leaves, but he was gaining experience all the time and becoming a little more critical of "unidentified flying objects."

The next day (September 16) he spent most of the morning feeding on the delicious nectar of the available flowers, though he did sun himself from time to time, gratefully absorbing the heat that was leading to his full development. In the early afternoon Lady Feigning crossed by his observation post, saw him, and swung upward into the sky at not too fast a pace, turning from time to time in graceful sweeps to display her wings and colors. Timorous's developing critical faculties told him that this was a female butterfly, but they were not acute enough to inform him that for a monarch she was remarkably small. Quickly he set off after the red-and-black deceiver, his sexual desires overcoming the more juvenile ones of just rushing about and feeding. He flew up after Lady Feigning in an aerial courtship dance. His main object was to get just above and a little ahead of her and then to drive her down to a landing on some surface, such as a leaf, rather in the way that a fighter or scout aircraft will force down a suspect plane to a landing. Flashing his wings he dodged backward and forward several times and gradually moved Lady Feigning toward a flat sumac leaf, on which he landed. Lady Feigning, in view of the urgency of her task, appeared to think that there was no point in wasting time on the senseless formalities of courtship and landed beside him.

Timorous then started the next stage in the courtship procedure. One way of stopping the female's rushing about was to secrete a perfume that would attract her. Timorous had a special apparatus for this purpose. He could curl the end of his abdomen upward, extrude some scent glands, and transfer a secretion from them to two receptor cups on the hind wings. In and by the cups were some special small, dark scales which absorbed the highly perfumed liquid. Quickly Timorous prepared himself, impregnated the special scales (known as androconia), and again took off after Lady Feigning, confident that his perfume and flashing shape would lead to the desired result. Circling round and round, he at last got above her and released a few scent scales. The effect was extraordinary. These scents are highly specialized. Timorous's was attractive only to female monarchs, and both the smell and his dance pattern immediately informed Lady Feigning that the attractive-looking male stranger was not of her species and therefore of no use to her. She at once went into an antimale routine. She flew off and Timorous followed her; alighting on a leaf she extruded her sex organs, not as an invitation to Timorous to mate with her but as an indication to him, by means of sight and smell, that he had made a mistake. She took off again and flew almost vertically upward, a flight pattern quite different from the darting, lively flight of courtship. Timorous went after her; he had not had much experience. She kept steadily on and up until he had to admit defeat. He fell back toward the milkweed patch, exhausted by his efforts. A few seconds later a vast blue cloud surrounded him, from which he could not escape. He had been captured in the entomologist's net. She labeled him with the number GF.2580, recorded the date September 16, and released him at once.

A few yards away the male viceroy, Two-tongues, was resting on a leaf, slowly opening and closing his wings and keeping a sharp lookout. He saw Lady Feigning fly by and rapidly set out after her. She at once noticed that this creature was different; not only was he slightly smaller but he also had a quite different flight pattern from that of the monarch she had just rejected. Two-tongues made quick wing strokes and went into short glides with his wings held horizontally. Timorous, though he had been excited and eager, beat his wings to a slower rhythm and made longer glides, holding his wings slightly downward. Had Lady Feigning not been so eager to secure the fertilizing sperm she would have noticed this different pattern immediately. Attracted by Two-tongues' correct behavior, Lady Feigning paused. Two-tongues got above her and released the proper viceroy scent. At once she became aware that this was the male she needed and entered into the aerial courtship dance that is a preparation for mating. Three or four minutes later the two copulated and soon Lady Feigning was looking for apple and willow foliage; on what she regarded as suitable leaves she laid fertile eggs.

In two days the viceroy eggs hatched to young caterpillars which rapidly progressed to the second instar stage. Then they immediately started to feed on the leaves in a special manner, adopted in order to form hibernacula—shelters in which to pass the winter. The caterpillars cut away the tissue of a suitable leaf on either side of the central rib from the tip to about halfway down. The little stalk left was then bent down and secured with silk and a glue that the caterpillar secreted. It then drew the edges of the leaf together, making a snug tube in which to pass the bad weather. The caterpillars prevent leaf fall by securing the hibernacula to the twigs with silk and glue and possibly also excrete a substance preventing the formation at the base of the leaf stalk of the leaf-fall hormone, a substance which normally leads to the production of an abscission layer of cork cells between the leaf stalk and the twig and the consequent fall of the leaf.

Two-tongues died from a fall in rough weather two days after mating and Lady Feigning died from exhaustion soon after her last egg was laid. In the spring the young caterpillars emerged from their shelters, fed on the budding leaves, and the cycle continued.

Returning to mimicry, the fact that particular butterflies have particular flight patterns is an argument against Batesian mimicry's being of much use to the mimic. One might easily suppose that what a butterfly can learn a bird can also learn; as a result the bird would know, either by inheritance over the generations or by direct experience, that the flight of the monarch indicated an unpleasant meal and that of the viceroy a good one.

Many entomologists can recognize insects from their flight, and the French author Colette wrote:

"When a butterfly is on the wing, at some distance, I do not see it so well, but I name it from its flight and its behavior. How, for example, can one mistake the rapid wing-beat of the swallowtail, or the majestic flight of the scarce zebra, that floats on the air apparently lifeless?" [10]

Since the beginning of September the entomologist and the student had raised some 600 adult monarchs and captured 200 in the neighborhood. All these had been labeled, numbered, and released. Among the captures on September 12 was Pliable and among those on September 16 Timorous, she becoming GF.2575 and he GF.2580. From time to time butterflies were released in batches of from ten to thirty, one batch in the morning and the other in the afternoon. The marked butterflies were conspicuous and quite a number of them were recaptured by the young couple themselves over the milkweed patch and among the flowering goldenrod. Encouraging as these re-encounters were, they were not of much importance. When children equipped with butterfly nets were watching, the couple postponed the release or carried the butterflies to a more remote spot. Sometimes they took a batch of butterflies out in a boat and freed them in the middle of Lake George. On one such occasion they noted that a butterfly which alighted on the water not only did not sink but could take off again.

OUT INTO THE WORLD

The monarchs were big enough and strong enough to overcome the surface drag of water on their wings. A few, however, were lost to fish.

Pliable was released at noon on September 12. Her first reaction was to get away as quickly as possible from the scene of the extraordinary happenings she had just experienced: confinement, apparently solid air (the glass of her cage), handling by a vast, strange-smelling creature, and finally the sudden appearance on her left forewing of a square white patch. Trees, bushes, and foliage could hide enemies, even that strange solid blue cloud; she decided to get high up in the air and survey the scene in safety. To do this she had to find a rising "thermal," a patch of warm air from a hot, dry piece of ground. Spreading her fine wings and beating them to their full extent, almost through a semicircle from high above her head to well below her body, she developed full speed and soon was over a piece of dried-up pasture. Her wings were now almost stilled; they gave a few leisurely gentle beats, the wing tips rising about half an inch from the horizontal and not sinking below it, as she glided over the patch and rose 300 feet in the air. She lost her nervousness as she found that the strange white object on her wing apparently did no harm. Far away she could see a pink patch bordered with gold and dropped back toward it, using the cruising stroke of her wings from time to time to avoid being blown off course by gusts of wind. Her speed and direction were controlled by the frequency and extent of the wing beats. Her journeying or jog-trot speed was obtained from a beat in which the wing tips traveled a distance of about 1 ¼ inches from a little below the horizontal upward. She steered by varying the length of the beat, reducing it on the side to which she wished to turn. Her escape zigzags were made by stopping the wings on one side for a moment and then beating them again as she stopped those on the other side. She could make very quick turns in this way, but on the whole she was quite fearless. Her instincts told her that birds would leave her alone; nevertheless her great eyes were always alert for danger. What she did not know was that the label altered her appearance. As she was descending, a blue jay was attracted by the white wing patch and darted up toward her. Pliable saw him coming. She stopped her starboard wings, turned rapidly to the right, tilted her hind wings downward, which moved her head down, and then went into her full-speed routine. As a result she went rapidly downward, and to the bird appeared to have disappeared into thin air. In the circumstances she had to fly downward. Just to have closed her wings and dropped would not have saved her. She was so light and had such a large surface area in comparison with her weight that she would merely have fluttered slowly to earth if she had let gravity act unaided.

Let us now consider this lovely, peaceful, beautiful, and well-balanced country scene, "where every prospect pleases and only man is vile." In fact all the different kinds of animals and plants are competing to their utmost for success, which is measured by multiplication and the extension of their species. Quite ruthlessly, even if quietly and slowly, they are seeking to dominate the scene, each for its own species. Plants fiercely compete with one another for air, light, space, and the water and plant foods in the soil. Shrubs spring up, spread out, and cut the light off from the grasses; trees grow and spread their leaves over the shrubs, eventually stifling them. Some plants dispense with the expensive process of forming rigid trunks or stems for themselves and clinging to trees climb to the light, regardless of the fact that they may eventually kill the supporting trees. The very leaves of a single plant compete with one another; the upper ones spread out and shade the lower ones, depriving them of light and thus of food. Animals eat the plants and prey on each other. Look at that pretty bird, how graceful, how charming. Being an early one, it dashes down and seizes a worm, drags it protesting—as far as a worm can protest—from its burrow, and gulps it into its crop. But observe more closely; the bird is constantly nervous. It turns its head left and right, up and down, and keeps moving this way and that, fearful of attack by some predator. A fox may jump from the bushes; a hawk fall from the sky. The whole life system is highly competitive from start to finish. It produces a degree of efficiency but at the cost of much cruelty. It is the state of nature; a state people tend to over-romanticize today. When psychological dangers are commonly more important than physical ones, there is a popular belief that a return to the natural world would be a great improvement. This seems to me to be a profound error. In spite of fierce competition between humans, the weakest going to the wall; in spite of wars, assassinations, and disasters, the present state of civilization, poor as it may be, is still far better than the state of nature.

Timorous and Pliable had been endowed with characteristics that did not call for much aggressive behavior on their part. Timorous had eaten an egg of his own kind, and both he and Pliable had extracted the poisonous and bad-tasting substances in the milkweed and by incorporating these in their own bodies had made themselves distasteful to predators. Nevertheless they were among the gentlest of the world's creatures. Even so, they had enemies that limited their indefinite expansion; diseases, particularly those of a virus nature, were a considerable brake on excessive population growth.[11]

Timorous was released in the afternoon of September 16. He at once climbed 20 feet into the air and relaxed on the reddening leaf of a sugar maple, slowly opening and closing his wings as if to assure himself that normal conditions prevailed. He spent the afternoon feeding and then sought out a secure shelter between two twigs for the night. At this time of year leaves were dangerous refuges, since during the night a leaf might drop, taking with it in its fall the sleeping monarch that grasped it. The ground also was dangerous. Under the trees lay a scattering of monarch and other wings dropped by shrews which had eaten the bodies of insects that had either fallen or taken up night quarters too close to the ground. The little animals left the indigestible wings; they did not seem to mind the bitter taste of the milkweed residues in the monarch bodies.

The next day Timorous, resting on a milkweed leaf after feeding, saw a monarch pass by; the insect was in fact male, but the difference in the appearance of the sexes is not great. Thinking it to be female, Timorous immediately set off after the stranger. The stranger too thought Timorous was a bold female in need of his attentions, a piece of vanity not confined to males of the butterfly world. Timorous maneuvered himself ahead of and slightly above the other butterfly, who immediately turned and did the same thing to Timorous. Then the "two males" dance started—a characteristic over-and-under movement as the two fluttered up and up into the sky. The weather being calm and sunny, both were releasing the male perfume from their scent glands, and both seemed to note that it was not having the effect it would have had on a female—that of inducing her to settle on a leaf or twig as a prelude to copulation. Exhausted by efforts that seemed to lead nowhere and at last cognizant that the smell in the air was wrong, Timorous broke off the dance and glided downward toward the milkweed patch once more. He devoted the next hour to feeding, replacing the precious fuel used up in the chase; he then set to watching and waiting again, slowly opening and closing his wings. Repeatedly he was disappointed. As on the day he was captured, he had become so anxious and enthusiastic that he would chase after almost anything that moved in the air. Once he went after a small bird, which turned and attacked him, catching the hinder part of his body in its beak. Timorous's leathery body resisted the short sharp peck; it was painful but no permanent harm was done. He later chased a mourning cloak butterfly and a red admiral, neither of them in the least like a monarch.

4 STARTING SOUTH

SEPTEMBER 12 – OCTOBER 8

In mid-September flowers well supplied with nectar were still abundant and though Pliable and Timorous fed eagerly they both were visibly restive. After emergence they flitted leisurely from flower to flower, full of confidence and calm, hardly moving their widespread wings. The future seemed to hold no problems and the air no enemies. Timorous's sex organs were still developing and his attempts at mating might be considered as training exercises; even if he had succeeded in finding a female monarch and keeping her still long enough to mate, it is doubtful whether he could have transferred any viable sperm. His courtship activities still included a considerable element of play. Pliable was not yet ready for sexual stimulation. This might be described as a pleasant, adolescent stage, in which they enjoyed good weather and plenty. Moving at random from one flower to another, they uncoiled their long mouths, inserted the tubes into the blossoms, and sucked up the honey so greatly needed for their future. In return they transferred pollen, thus aiding cross-fertilization of the milkweeds. After feeding they would lazily fly off in any direction, sun themselves with open wings, close and open their wings from time to time, and finally drift slowly to another blossom. The push and pull of selection have made flowers produce attractive honey, whetting the appetites of insects to induce them to go on feeding on the same sort of flower, for it would be no profit to the plant for a monarch or a bee to transfer pollen from, say, milkweed to blackberry.

Later in September the flight pattern of Pliable and Timorous became directional; they were still feeding and moving from one site to another, but more often than not the move was south or southwest by south, in the general direction of Albany or Gloversville. They did not spend as much time resting or sunning themselves as they had earlier.

This change and the general disturbance of their peaceful routine was a reaction caused by the southward-moving sun, colder nights, and a shorter period of warmth each day. In spite of an ample food supply they seemed to know instinctively that a bad time was coming.

A varying day length is of great importance in biology. Some plants will flower only if the duration of daylight is lengthening day by day; others, such as chrysanthemums, only if it is shortening. One of the triumphs of applied science is the ability to get chrysanthemums to flower all the year round; by investing some $200,000 one can cover an acre of land with glass and automatic blinds and by manipulating the blinds make the plants "think" the days are shortening and bring them into bloom in April.

That Pliable, Timorous, and the rest of the monarchs were aware that the days were getting shorter is remarkable, for the shortening as the fall advances is only about 3 minutes a day; about

0.2 percent a day or 0.4 percent of the daylight hours. A human can scarcely notice such a small change. If you saw two movies on successive days, could you say if one was 3 minutes longer than the other? If you could you would be noticing a difference of 3 percent, seven times more than that spotted by Timorous. Animals can do many things beyond human ken. Nevertheless, humans do notice the shortening days because their memories compare current observation with that of, say, a week ago. The difference is then 20 minutes. And humans also have watches.

The monarchs can either spot a 0.4 percent change in day length or can remember more distant days and compare those with the present. Perhaps they can do both by means of some mechanism acquired by the operation of thousands and thousands of generations. The shortening day effect was also reinforced by the falling temperature; as the sun sank in the sky, the time taken to warm the morning air to about 55 degrees F. increased, so that the shortening day effect was magnified. So was the difference in the time of sunrise. The difference in the time of sunrise between September 1 and September 28 is 28 minutes. Now if it took an hour to heat the air sufficiently for a monarch to move on September 1 it would take, say, two hours to do so on September 24, so that the apparent difference between the two dates to the butterfly would be not 28 minutes but one hour and 28 minutes— the actual difference plus the extra hour for warming the air at the later date.

In their own instinctive way the monarchs in the midst of plenty were taking thought for the morrow and in fact survived in greater numbers than those who did not. Although they could have withstood freezing temperatures for a short while, they could not, like some butterflies (the red admiral is one) have supported them for a whole winter. The monarchs survive by migrating.

THE YEAR OF THE BUTTERFLY

Had Jean de La Fontaine, the seventeenth-century French poet, known the monarch butterfly he could better have used that creature instead of the grasshopper in his fable. The grasshopper, in actual fact, is rather more sensible than the ant and passes the winter as an egg. In the remote past the race of monarchs that did not prepare for winter in time simply perished; nothing is known of them.

The migration of the monarchs started in a leisurely way; it was hardly noticeable to begin with. By September 15 a general southerly direction could be observed in the fluttering of the monarchs over the milkweed. September 20 was a great day for the student entomologist. Watching a varied collection of butterflies feeding on the Buddleia flowers in a friend's garden at Corinth, New York, she suddenly saw a monarch with a label on it. Slowly she stalked the creature; moving her butterfly net gradually forward she kept it low and with a sudden upward thrust and quick twist captured the insect—No. GF.2580 (in fact, Timorous) , which she had herself labeled and released four days ago at Glens Falls. The recapture was most encouraging. Obviously the insect had been moving southwest at a rate of about 3 miles a day. She noted the event in her records and released the insect, whispering, "Fly, fly, fly south, my pretty boy," and wishing she could go too.

To be surrounded twice in a week by a solid, bluish cloud from which there was no escape must be a shattering sensation; Timorous was not conditioned to this particular experience. He had an ingrained pattern telling him to avoid large, smelly, warm animals (mammals) and bulky moving objects, but none for dealing with glass and fine netting. A few kinds of insects may be learning to deal with the former, but the monarchs are not among them. Summer flies of many kinds batter, batter, and batter against a glass window, hopelessly trapped until they are killed by flyspray, swatter, or spider or fall dead exhausted by lack of food and water. A few flies, such as the cluster flies (*Pollenia* species) and some bluebottles, after a while give up battering against the glass and fly away seeking another way out; often they are successful. The cluster flies are looking for earthworms, and most of the bluebottles for carrion on which to lay eggs. Perhaps a gene for dealing with glass is being selected out, or possibly the smell of damp earth or dead flesh guides these flies to an open door or some other exit.

All Timorous could do in the net was to flutter and to make a dart for any opening he saw. But he was not in the net for long, and once free he was soon flying southwest again, at a slightly increased speed.

As twilight came on he sought a refuge for the night; the ideal spot would be sheltered from wind, rain, and enemies, and not likely to fall down. Consequently he avoided the broad-leaved trees; their leaves might drop off during the night. Unlike some butterflies, he had no sucker pads on his feet and had to hook the last joints of his legs over some narrow structure such as a thin stem or leaf stalk, or over the serrations of a leaf edge. He found a pine tree, hooked the claws of his second pair of legs over some needles on the southwest side, and having anchored himself securely opened his wings to the last rays of the setting sun. He slowly opened and closed them several times as if to show his satisfaction with the place, and this activity attracted a few more monarchs, which settled near him as if for protection.

On September 21, as the sun warmed the air, the monarchs left one by one, Timorous being the last. He spent the early hours feeding and slowly drifting south. The nectar he sucked up consisted mostly of sugar with a few additional ingredients, such as vitamins. The sugar provided the fuel for his flight; some of it was converted to fat, which was, in effect, his reserve fuel tank. It was stored in his body and would be called on at a later date. Fat as a long-distance fuel is superior to carbohydrates such as glycogen, since it is stored free of water and, weight for weight, supplies about eight times as much energy.[1]

The flapping of wings in flight is a great user of energy. The wings alternately start, move, stop, and reverse and thus have all the disadvantages of the orthodox internal combustion engine, the pistons of which do the same thing. Timorous in flight consumed fat at a rate of about 1 percent of his body weight per hour: this compares favorably with a jet-engine aircraft, which uses fuel at about 12 percent of its total weight per hour, but the relative speeds are vastly different. Mechanically the jet is much more efficient; the efficiency of Timorous was low. Only about 15 percent of the fuel he consumed appeared as work done: the rest was lost as heat.[2]

Timorous had left Corinth in a generally southwesterly direction. By noon he and his companions reached the shores of the great Sacandaga Reservoir. They did not appear to like the idea of crossing so much open water, for they rose in the air and turned along the shoreline, eventually flying about 20 feet above it. From time to time Timorous came down to feed on aster and milkweed flowers. As the sun set he roosted with his fellows. The weather was fine and a gentle breeze from the northeast had helped them along.

By now Timorous was quite self-confident. Birds hardly bothered him; parasites attack only the egg or caterpillar stages, not adult butterflies. Diseases could injure him, but of this he was not aware. Dangers were present on the ground, but by a winged creature the ground can be largely ignored; he was seldom there. But "pride goeth before destruction and an haughty spirit before a fall."

Many animals establish territories and seek to exclude others, particularly those of their own species, from them. Birds are very territory-conscious. The main reason a male bird sings is to proclaim his territory, to warn off other males, and then to attract a suitable female for breeding purposes. The territory is a device which limits population growth and makes the best use of available resources. Territories are also known, but to a lesser extent, in the insect world. On the morning of September 24 Timorous, flying southwest along the slopes of Kittatinny Mountain near Blairstown, New Jersey, crossed into an area which a small buckeye butterfly (*Junonia coenia*) apparently considered his exclusive property. The buckeye, although only half Timorous's size, rushed at him, bent on the destruction of the invader. Timorous had never experienced anything like this. The buckeye had come straight up from below. Timorous turned quickly to the right. The buckeye rose above him, then, diving, flashed past him, holding his wings open and still for an instant to expose the eye spots, then concealing the spots again by subsequent rapid movements of his wings. The sudden exposure of these spots frighten many creatures; they are used by many insects, particularly Lepidoptera, as a defense mechanism. Three rushes of this sort were too much for Timorous; utterly defeated in spite of his size, he withdrew. He flew farther west and then turned south, avoiding the buckeye's territory and seeking to avoid the bad luck of the "evil eye" flashed on him by the sinister *Junonia*.

The eye spot, or ocellus, on the wing, according to Caillois, exerts a strange psychological power, similar to one exerted by the steady stare of a pair of eyes, man or owl. The ocelli are not frightening because they resemble eyes: eyes are frightening because they are like ocelli.[3]

As day succeeded day, Timorous continued to move southwest, to some extent losing his sex urge, for he no longer darted so often after moving objects as possible mates. He fed frequently but spent shorter and shorter intervals in sunning and resting. He was now nearly always flying in the company of other monarchs, and usually they roosted together at night. By flying high over Baltimore they reached the neighborhood of Stevenson, Maryland, on October 8.

Pliable meanwhile had taken another route. After she had been labeled and released at Glens Falls on September 12 she had headed in fright for the first piece of open sky that showed, which had happened to be to the east. In full-powered flight—almost a 180-degree beat of her wings—she rose rapidly in the air, circled once or twice, then glided down again to a patch of flowering blackberries, asters, and milkweed at Hudson Falls. After that she traveled due south, appearing to have a fix both on the Hudson River and on the New York Central railroad track. The latter was the better guide, for the ties of the track made a comforting pattern in her complex eyes. Her flight style was similar to that of Timorous—feeding on flowers and passing from one to another usually, though not always, in a southerly direction. Whenever she came over the railroad she held to it, turning south and following it until drawn away by the sight of flowers or the setting of the sun. As an immature virgin female she preferred solitary shelter for the night and did not join the mass of males and mated females on tree roosts which is such a familiar sight. Usually she clung upside down on a low bush, avoiding as Timorous did the changing leaves (for she could grasp the leaf stalks or serrated edges such as those of maple leaves) .

STARTING SOUTH

Pliable's immature state and virginity were assets; she could concentrate on feeding and flight and need not worry about mating. Occasionally she had to discourage males by using an antimale routine of the type Lady Feigning had used on Timorous.

Day after day the pattern continued, each day a little longer time being devoted to flying and less idling and display. But Pliable still spent almost as much time every day in feeding, both to provide fuel for the southward flight and to fill her "storage tank" with fat. The successful campaigner must secure his reserves in good time before undertaking any great expedition, and Pliable, though she did not know it, had 2,000 miles to go, a flight comparable for her to a man's getting to the moon and back. The southerly direction had been imprinted on her by the chance of finding herself above the railroad track and the Hudson River soon after the marking trauma, and she continued in this direction. It should be emphasized that she was not moving toward a perceived goal but was leaving an area which, as she was instinctively aware, would soon be unsuitable for her. Nevertheless, she appeared to be deliberately going south, to safe winter weather. The student who had wished Timorous (GF.2580) a happy journey was under the same impression.

By September 15 Pliable had reached Albany and increasing her daily mileage reached Wappingers Falls by September 18. She journeyed with a number of other monarchs coming down from Canada, Maine, and Vermont but usually continued to spend the night alone. An exception was the night of September 16 which was wet and stormy; on this occasion she settled on the southwest side of a pine tree with about thirty other monarchs, all packed closely together for protection. During the night and the next day the wind dropped; as the temperature rose above 50 degrees F. the monarchs left the roost in twos and threes and set off again.

Pliable regulated her speed and direction by what she saw of the ground below and the sun above her. But in relation to speed, air movement—winds—must first be considered. Anything flying in moving air, whether it be bird, insect, or airplane, moves with that air, no matter in what direction the animal or aircraft is pointing. If the machine or animal hovers (as does a balloon or a hummingbird moth), it is in a dead calm whatever the speed of the air as the object is moving with and as part of the air. A passenger in a balloon in a steady 60-mile-an-hour gale is still in a dead calm, but usually the wind is gusty, so the passenger might feel a few jolts from the gusts as the speed changes. Eighteenth-century balloonists did not understand this and so mounted enormous sails on their balloons in the hope of navigating them. These were quite useless; balloon and sails were all part of the air and moved with it.

The same thing happens at sea. The vessel moves with the current no matter what way the ship is pointing, and to find out the direction an airplane or ship is really going a calculation well known to seamen and pilots must be made—this is called the triangle of velocities. The direction the ship is pointing is the course; this is plotted on a piece of paper on a scale in proportion to its speed, say 10 miles per hour (see diagram at left on page 67). Let us suppose that it is headed due south and there is a current from the northeast of 5 miles per hour. A line AB of 10 units (equal to 10 miles) is drawn vertically, and another line BC of 5 units is drawn to represent the speed and direction of the current from the northeast. The points CA are then joined and this line will show the actual movement of the ship, known as its track, and the speed, in this case 14 miles per hour. If the captain wishes to travel due south under these conditions he must "lay off" his course to the east by an amount equal to the angle $C'A'B'$ to get

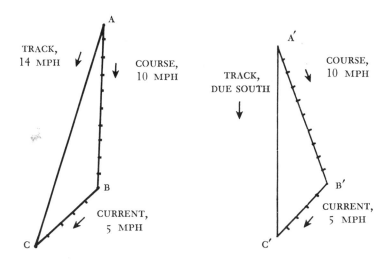

the situation shown in the diagram at right. The same rule applies to all moving objects; if the medium in which the object is situated is moving, the object moves with it. If the object is a thinking being it may scarcely be aware of the movement—the drift—just as the balloon passenger is unaware of movement unless he can see the ground. If on a good road going west to east at the equator you drive a car at 70 miles per hour you might consider you were traveling at a fair speed, but in fact it is nothing to the speed at which you are really traveling, for the earth is turning from west to east at that point at a speed of about 1,000 miles per hour. But unless you make a special effort to recall this point you are unaware of it; you have no near-enough reference point. The sun and the stars are too far away. The passenger in an aircraft usually does not know that most of the time the machine's track is different from its course, or heading, but the pilot is constantly conscious of it and takes advantage of favorable winds to economize fuel and shorten the time of the journey. This effect sometimes can be seen from the ground; a slow-flying aircraft with a strong wind at right angles to its course can actually be seen to be moving somewhat crabwise and not in the direction in which it is pointing. The winds are a most important factor in insect migration. The methods these creatures use to deal with them have fascinated naturalists for years.

The air in which Pliable was flying was usually moving one way or another and she adjusted her course to keep her direction almost due north/south along the railroad line. She adjusted the height of her flight according to the direction and strength of the winds. Near the ground, wind force is lessened by the interference of trees, bushes, and buildings; this zone is called the boundary layer.[4] Naturally the layer varies in depth according to the nature of ground and the speed of the wind; it may be a few inches or more than 30 feet. When the wind was against her, Pliable dropped into the boundary layer so as to lessen its effects, and when it favored her adhesion to her imprinted track she rose out of it and let the wind help her. If the wind in the boundary layer was stronger than her flying speed and she was flying into it she would be carried backward; as soon as this happened she would stop flying and seek shelter on the leeward side of some tree or bush until conditions were favorable again. All the time she was watching the ground beneath her and the sun above. When she was flying a retinal image of the ground passed over her eyes from front to back. Since she could not move her eyes, in order to see something outside her range of vision she had to turn her whole body, a factor which actually assisted her navigation. The speed at which the ground pattern image passed over her retina depended on her height above ground, her flying speed, and the speed and direction of the wind. The higher she was, the slower was the speed of the images over her retina. She had a preferred retinal velocity—that is to say, there was a certain speed at which she liked the images of the ground below to pass over her eyes.[5] Pliable's figure was 7 miles per hour at a height of about 20 feet.

The kind of image on the retina of an insect can be greatly influenced by the nature of the ground. A plowed field will give a very satisfactory pattern, a calm lake scarcely any image at all—no doubt this is one reason that monarchs do not like to fly over water. The image given by a rough or roughish sea with "white horses" on it is good but unsatisfactory because the white horses themselves are moving. Railroad tracks, telephone lines, and power lines provide excellent markers for migrating monarchs. Pliable found the New York Central track from Hudson Falls to New York City particularly useful because it ran in the direction she wanted and the regularly spaced crossties gave an ideal image on her retina—a far better background than one of trees, hedges, roads, rocks, houses, and fields. Had she known what caused it, she could well have been grateful to that strange animal, man, for laying out this long, well-marked path in the right direction for the sole benefit of monarchs seeking escape from an approaching winter.

Pliable also checked her position by the sun when it could be seen or sensed. To use the sun to maintain a direction one must either know the time or be able to measure the sun's elevation over the horizon, in the latter case making allowances for the time of year and the latitude of the place one is in. Pliable certainly used the sun as a navigation aid. In order to keep her flight direction constant, as the sun moved across the September sky in its daily course, she had to alter the angle of her body to the sun through an arc of about 180 degrees in any one day and to do that she had to be aware of the time of day. For instance, if she was flying southwest, the sun had to be at 45 degrees on her left wing at noon, dead ahead at 3 p.m., and at 45 degrees on her right wing as it set. Her built-in clock was operated by the state of her muscles, her tiredness, her digestion, and certain glands. When she was very tired she knew it was late, that the sun was low, and that it should be to her right, and to achieve this she would alter course, thus insuring that she would continue in a southwesterly direction.

Naturalists have always speculated as to how the monarchs find their way. First, it must be remembered that by no means all of them do. Although thousands of monarchs are seen in the southern states and in Mexico and observers marvel at them, these are only a surviving remnant of those that set out. Perhaps half or more perish on the journey. The monarchs must take advantage of several systems in order to make the trip. The most important of these is the wind; they are mainly flying ahead of a cold front coming southwest. But since they are not always flying directly with the wind, they need to navigate as well. They are able to do this by using the sun as their reference point, compensating as it moves. There is also the possibility that they use as a guide the height of the sun over the horizon—that is, its angle of elevation. If Pliable were doing this she would have to know the approximate date and the approximate latitude she was in. She would know the date from the flowers available and from the weather, particularly the temperature. Knowing the date, she would then have some idea of the latitude from the arc the sun makes from sunrise to sunset and the height it reaches over the horizon. She can then know that the sun will rise to a certain point (the zenith) at noon and consequently if it is only halfway there the time is a certain number of hours before or after noon and the line from her to the sun is either southeast (morning) or southwest (afternoon). From this knowledge she can set her southwest course. One can assume that she would know if it were morning or afternoon from the

tiredness she was experiencing or from the actual movement of
the sun up or down. If she had happened to be at Albany, New
York (43 degrees north), on September 21 (the equinox) —
though in fact she got there on September 15—the sun at noon
would be about 47 degrees above the horizon. The sun would have
risen at 5:44 a.m. (Eastern Standard Time) and would set at 5:48
p.m., thus passing through an arc of about 180 degrees during the
day. If at a certain point she noticed the sun was 25 degrees over
the horizon and still rising, she would then know it was in the
southeast and that to keep a southwesterly direction she must set
her track at 90 degrees to the direction of the sun. This is in effect
navigating on the direction of the sun: its height is a confirmation
and an indication of her latitude. The fact that the sun is about 47
degrees over the horizon at noon (or 25 degrees at 8:50 a.m.)
means she must be in latitude 43 degrees north, that of Albany. If
the sun were at 55 degrees over the horizon at noon she would
know she was at latitude 35 degrees north, the latitude of
Chattanooga, Tennessee. Men use instruments, reason, and the
phraseology of reason in place of the instructive mechanisms of
the butterfly. The monarchs, obviously, do not calculate in degrees
and cardinal points, but they "get there just the same"—at least a
considerable number of them get there.

A similar theory on bird navigation was proposed by the British
author and ornithologist George V. T. Matthews. He postulated
that birds observed the movements of the sun over a short period
and were thus able to deduce the whole arc of its movement for
that day. They could then estimate its height at noon and the
latitude in which they were situated. Longitude is more important
for birds than for monarchs, and Matthews thought that birds
could also measure the azimuth of the sun—the angle from the
north to a point on the horizon projected vertically to meet the

line of sight, observer to sun, which would give the longitude.[6] It seems a great deal for a bird brain to do—to measure movement and two angles while flying—and even more for a butterfly, yet it is remarkable what creatures can do with simple devices. The fact that we would find the calculation impossible without elaborate instruments does not mean that monarchs could not use some system of this sort.

Pliable and her companions reached Peekskill by September 20, after which she began to feel a little confused. A day's journey south—about 10 miles—brought her to Verplanck, a place where the railroad tracks turned southeast and the river widened. Abandoning the railroad track and steering due west by the sun, she went out over the water for a short while, but the sun had nearly set and the air was cooling. Her reaction to cold overrode her instinct to move south, so she turned at right angles over the water and flew southeastward to the shore, where, along with some eighty more monarchs, she found a roost in the splendid gardens of Lyndhurst House, on the Hudson at Tarrytown, New York.

The next morning was sunny and Pliable fed for a while, then rose to a considerable height and circled around to get her bearings. She found the railroad track again, and since it was so imprinted on her memory, she started to fly south along it once more. By the time she got south of Yonkers she was again troubled. The ground pattern passing over her eyes was a difficult one; there were many roads, houses, rail tracks, and a strange set of mountains ahead emitting sulfurous smells; a constantly rising mass of hot air was being wafted northeast by a southwesterly wind. Somewhat confused, she let herself be carried northeastward by this current, eventually coming down to roost near Norwalk, Connecticut. Next day, September 22, she appeared to be determined to go south no matter what. In spite of her distaste for water, she moved out over Long Island Sound, coming over land once more at Smithtown, Long Island, where she found purple asters on which to feed. Then she set off south again and soon came to the seashore. There she joined a large flock of monarchs coming down from New England and Canada. They all kept to the shoreline, and though certain individuals would drop out to feed from time to time, the flight was now much more purposeful. Several thin streams of monarchs, moving in directions ranging from south to southwest by west, at rates of two or three per five minutes on a front of 50 yards, now began to fuse together. A thin stream is hardly noticed as a migration unless a trained observer is deliberately watching. However, as the streams joined, the numbers were sufficient to be noticed by the human inhabitants, who gathered to stare at and admire the passage of lavishly colored butterflies all day long.

The swarm moved along the southern spur of Jamaica Bay— Rockaway Beach—and out over Lower Bay to land in New Jersey at Sandy Hook on September 23. The sea was comparatively calm and made little pattern on Pliable's eyes. The reactions of monarchs to flying over open water and over land are different. Over water, in spite of the wind's direction, they appear always to be flying toward the south or southwest. What in fact occurs is this: Over the water and with a wind from the north, some of the monarchs might head north into the wind at, say, 7 miles per hour. Some would fly high, in order to get a good retinal picture, and a few would fly low. The high fliers flying into a wind of, say, 10 miles per hour (which is not much of a wind) would actually be moving backward at 3 miles per hour ($10 - 7 = 3$). The few low fliers in the boundary layer might make progress against the wind and reach land. The land features give a better picture on their eyes, and they rise in the air, leave the boundary layer, and are subjected to the full wind force and carried backward—that is, to the south. Eventually these turn around and go with the wind at $10 + 7 = 17$ miles per hour. The pattern on their eyes would now be moving too fast, so they come down into the boundary layer, where the wind is less strong, and reduce their southward speed. This descent also has the advantage of enabling them to see flowers and they could pause to feed and refuel their systems.

With a wind from the south over land the monarchs kept low in the boundary layer and made some progress against the wind. Over water they would rise, be carried northward, and eventually come to the land/water boundary. Here they would drop low again, turn, and make southward progress into the wind until they reached the water again, when the process would be repeated. Some might stay low over the water, making a little progress southward. At this time of the year most of the winds are from the north or northeast, heralding the approach of winter: the monarchs appeared to be forewarned of it. Successive generations over the millennia had become conditioned to react in this way and thus to survive.

Pliable was one of the flight of monarchs heading southwest over Lower Bay and she flew comparatively low to reach the New Jersey coast. There the swarm went inland and split into two main streams, one keeping along the shore and the other, which included Pliable, finding the Pennsylvania Railroad track and moving southwest over Philadelphia, Wilmington, and Baltimore. Any building in their way was circumvented by altering course at right angles and turning again to resume the original direction. The number of monarchs was large enough that year to attract the attention of the press and hearten a public fearful that pesticides and industrial effluents were about to put an end to butterflies.[7]

STARTING SOUTH

In the past there have been times when swarms of monarchs frightened people. In the fall of 1892 the mayor and board of health of Cleveland, Ohio, were much concerned to prevent cholera entering the city. They set up an inspection station on the railroad at Glenville and any person thought to be infected was removed from the train. The "germ theory" of disease was new then, and apparently some of the people in Cleveland had very little idea of what germs were like. On September 19, 1892, vast swarms of monarchs began to appear over the city, flying down the southern shore of Lake Erie and also directly across the lake. While most Clevelanders were fascinated by the sight, some were alarmed, thinking the butterflies were cholera germs. The *Plain Dealer* for September 20, 1892, had a story with the following headlines:

SWARMS OF BUTTERFLIES INVADED CLEVELAND

And Everybody Gazed at the Wonderful Sight—A Beautiful Vision of Orange Yellow—Strange Flight of the Insects From North to South— Mistaken for Cholera Germs—Immigrants Who Disregarded Mayor Rose's Proclamation.

Apparently Mayor Rose, in view of the cholera threat, had prohibited human immigrants from entering the city. The story continues with an interesting account of a two-hour flow of millions of monarchs. They struck into Superior Street "over the Arcade building." "A living, breathing, palpitating picture. . . . But splendid as it was the disordered public mind mistook the beautiful visitors for cholera germs, disguised of course, for the

75

devil himself assumes a very pleasing form at times." Many people tried to "shoo" the butterflies back as they approached "too near the sacred soil of Cleveland." Needless to say, "shooing" had no effect. Nor did the wind: "The butterflies seemed unmindful of the stiff breeze that was blowing and wafting the flock in an undulating motion from one side of the street to the other, but continued their journey from the east to the southwest with a fair degree of speed."

The reporter consulted a local entomologist who seems to have given a cautious and mainly accurate account of the insect. He evidently believed that the flight was a migration—under the circumstances it would have been difficult to doubt it. But at that time many people thought that monarchs hibernated in hollow trees. Hollow trees are popular in the mythology of natural history and have served to "solve" many difficult problems.

The newspaper, and thus presumably the entomologist, called the insect a tropical butterfly but one found every season in Canada—a rather elastic definition of "tropical." The monarch's Latin name was only slightly misspelled—in all an accurate and interesting account of a monarch swarm.[8]

The undulating motion of the swarm from side to side of Superior Street indicates that the insects were being wafted this way and that by the breeze which rose and fell as they were watched: it provides another clue as to how the monarchs orientate and maintain their track. The triangle of velocities already discussed applies, but most of the thinking about its application to animal flight has been done either by seamen or by people thinking in terms of sea currents. An important characteristic of such currents is that their speed does not change very rapidly; they flow at the same speed and in the same direction for a considerable time and distance. The main characteristic of a wind is that its speed, and usually its direction, are constantly changing: a look at a registering wind gauge or weathercock shows that. This flow of wind around an average figure is not of much importance to airline pilots (except at times when landing) as the plane moves so rapidly. But it can be important at low speeds. In the diagram below the wind is entered at 5 miles per hour from the northeast and plotted as such, but actually wind would vary from, say, 10 miles per hour to dead calm (0) and from northeast by north to northeast by east, making its average speed and direction 5 miles per hour from the northeast. If the insect's course is due south and its air speed 10 miles per hour, several tracks are possible, among them numbers 1, 2, 3, and 4, as shown in the diagram. The average track, shown by the heavy line, is number 1.

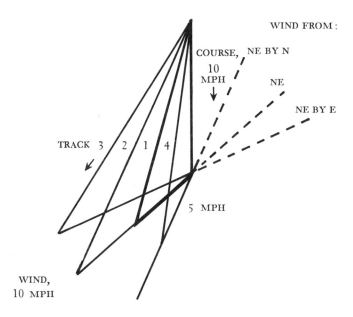

The butterfly's true direction is southwest by south, but, as a butterfly always moves with the wind (being part of the wind), the track will vary from due south to southwest with the varying wind, unless the creature alters its course. But as it is part and parcel of the wind, can it know that the wind speed has changed? Yes, or, rather, possibly yes. A butterfly, light as it is, has a certain momentum when flying. Newton's second law states that a moving body will continue to move at the same speed and in the same direction until something stops it. Things usually stop moving bodies pretty quickly: air friction, a brick wall, the body a bullet finds—examples can be multiplied. When the wind changes, the butterfly's momentum carries it forward for a fraction of a second in the same direction it was going. This change might well be sensed by the insect which could then adjust its course to maintain the same direction over the ground (its track) . Pliable in fact felt these changes as the lightest of wind puffs on her antennae, first on one side, then on the other; she moved to compensate for them and also to keep the retinal image direction standard and comfortable.

5 DANGEROUS JOURNEY

OCTOBER 8 – DECEMBER 18

When last observed, on October 8, Timorous had reached Stevenson, Maryland. He was a day or so ahead of Pliable. In the parklike grounds of the private estate Timberlane, he found flowers on which to feed and good roosting sites. The garden there contains a large black iron sculpture by Alexander Calder, which caught the rays of the setting sun and was warmed as a result. The warmth proved attractive to the monarchs, and Timorous and many of his companions clung to the rough edges of the iron. They made a startling patch on the black, of a dead-leaf color—the underside of the wings only being shown, as they roosted with wings closed. The patch attracted much attention from humans in the area. It moved and flashed to some extent as the butterflies opened their wings from time to time to catch the last light and moved to try and improve their hold on the sculpture. It was as though they did not approve of the late Calder statue, solid and immobile, and were trying to turn it into one of his early mobiles, which would flash and glitter. As people watched fascinated and dusk fell, a few late fireflies came out, flashing their various sex signals and adding to the strangeness of the scene. This flashing is another example of insects' achieving naturally something for which man needs complicated apparatus. Fireflies flash different signals to convey different messages, as does man with the Morse code. Mostly the flashes are by females to attract the male, each species having its own particular signal. However, *Photurus* can mimic the flash code of the female *Photinus*, thus attracting the male *Photinus*. *Photurus* is carnivorous; having attracted a male *Photinus* she eats him.

The sculpture was a poor site; though the black iron heated up quickly it also cooled quickly and soon the monarchs were immobile with cold. They attempted to move closer together for support as the iron cooled, and in doing so some fell to the ground. In the morning the severe black of the sculpture displayed a blazing patch of orange-red color as the butterflies opened their wings to the sun. As the monarchs took to flight, setting off southwest once more by twos and threes, the color gradually faded away.

Delightful as Timberlane was, Timorous was aware that he had not yet reached his winter quarters. He was informed of this by the height of the sun each day at its zenith, its warmth, and the temperature at night. Day after day he continued southwest—a steady routine of flying, feeding, riding the winds, and noting the highest point the sun reached before it sank again in the sky. In effect, he was engaged in a race with the sun. If he was to reach a warm climate for the winter, the sun must be a certain height above the horizon to bring about the conditions he needed. The sun at noon is sinking in the fall (and rising in the spring) at the rate of 2.6 degrees of latitude a day. A degree of latitude is about

68 miles, so the sun was "going south" at this time of year at a
rate of approximately 180 miles a day, a distance Timorous could
not hope to achieve under normal circumstances. With a good
"norther" and his own efforts he might occasionally make a day's
journey of that length, but even then, as far as the height of the
sun went, he would be only holding his own. Fly, fly as he might
the sun gained on him, drawing ever farther away. Also, he was
not flying due south but southwest, making the daily loss of sun
height yet greater.

It was to a considerable extent Timorous's instinct to seek a
wintering place where the sun at noon was about 50 degrees above
the horizon that drove him on. Not all races of monarchs have
this same requirement. Some are content with a lesser sun height
for winter quarters, and these would stop at higher latitudes, in
such famous monarch spots as Lighthouse Point, Florida (30
degrees north) or, for monarchs flying down the Pacific Coast,
Pacific Grove, California (36 degrees north).

Food and water were also important to Timorous, and he would
test flowers, raindrops, and even puddles to see if they were
suitable. He was far more sensitive than man to certain substances,
particularly to some sugars. As noted already, the monarchs need
sugar for the southward flight and can recognize incredibly low
concentrations of it, undetectable by the human tongue for that
purpose. Their sense of taste is in the tarsi of the middle pair of
legs. The tarsi are the next-to-last segments of the legs and roughly
correspond to the bones in the first posterior tarsals of the human
foot.

Sense organs located in different parts of the body from those
in which they occur in humans may seem strange, but the
arrangements have considerable advantages for butterflies. To
have continually to unroll and roll up their long tongues in order

to taste food would be time-consuming and cause much wear on that delicately coiled instrument. The hearing organs, in effect ears, may be located on the thorax, or forward part of the abdomen.[1] The eyes are always on the head. Some animals, such as snails, have eyes on stalks and can swivel them around. While this may be beneficial from some points of view, the creature loses the advantage of binocular vision, by means of which distances can be judged. Two fixed eyes act as a range finder; the different images on the two retinas provide an idea of how far away an object is. A snail may see food, but having no accurate idea of distance, it can waste much time trying to reach a meal which in reality is too distant to be worth bothering about. Humans are fortunate in being able to move their heads on their necks as well as their eyes in their sockets. The butterfly with its very large eyes has a wide field of vision, but to examine anything outside this it must turn its whole body, which it does not do often.

The sense of smell is located in the monarch's antennae. They have no lungs; air diffuses through their spiracles and along the air channels throughout the body, which absorb oxygen and give out carbon dioxide. The senses of smell and touch are very important in adult monarchs, particularly the females. Not only did Pliable have to find the same kinds of flowers for food as did Timorous, she would in due course also have to locate suitable sites for egg-laying. To that end she had more spines on the tibia (the section of the leg corresponding to human shin bones) of her hind legs than did Timorous.

Scudder pointed out an instance in which butterflies were better botanists than men. The caterpillars of some butterflies fed on different species of Solanaceae (the family that includes the potatoes and tomatoes) and those of an allied butterfly, *Thyridia*, fed on *Brunfelsia*, which plant was placed by botanists in the Scrophulariaceae. But George Bentham and J. D. Hooker, the great English botanists of the Victorian age, subsequently found that classification to be an error and moved *Brunfelsia* to the Solanaceae where, as the butterflies had been trying to indicate by their feeding habits, it had belonged all the time.[2]

Specialized feeding of necessity means sensitive organs to find and identify the particular food needed. It is achieved by means of hairs called sensory setae, which grow in cuplike pits on the body. The setae are usually hollow and are always connected with the nervous system so that the messages they are receiving can be acted upon.

Leaving Manassas, Virginia, on October 9, Timorous further increased his speed and roosted with greater numbers of his fellows. The swarm also flew in closer formation, and a few butterflies of other species joined it, such as the thistle or painted lady (*Vanessa cardui*), the large cloudless sulphur butterfly (*Phoebis sennae eubule*), and the little sulphur (*Terias lisa*) that itself sometimes flies in immense swarms.[3] The whole swarm continued to move southwest.

By October 10 Timorous was over Orange, Virginia, while Pliable, coming down the coast, was near Manteo, Roanoke Island, North Carolina, the place where the first American butterfly was painted by a European. The butterfly was a swallowtail (*Papilio thoas*), and the painter was John White, one of Sir Walter Raleigh's colonists from England who landed at Roanoke Island in 1585. The captain of the vessel stayed on the island for some weeks while the party established itself, and during this time Mr. White painted pictures, including the one of the butterfly. The captain took it back to London gave it to Thomas Mouffet, who used it in his book. The painting is now in the British Museum, along with Mouffet's manuscript, but the colony on Roanoke Island disappeared and its fate has never been known.

Continuing down the foot of the southeast side of the Blue Ridge Mountains Timorous and his companions began to travel in larger and larger swarms. One rough night near Lexington, North Carolina, many of them were massed together on a branch of a pine tree on its lee side, the southwest side, as the sun set. The position and nature of the tree attracted more and more butterflies and at about 6: 30 p.m. the not very strong branch broke, throwing 600 monarchs onto the ground. Most of the butterflies, among them Timorous, managed to regain the tree, for fortunately the wind had dropped with the setting sun; even so a hundred or more were lost, either having their wings damaged in the fall or, not finding a safe enough roost for the night, being eaten by predators. A telltale scatter of wings beneath the tree told the story; the wings, being of little food value, were left. The losses were soon made up by the addition of new recruits picked up as the swarm moved southwest. At Charlotte, North Carolina, Timorous got a fix on the railroad running southwest, which increased his speed.

Monarchs were migrating along this general route long before man, Indian or European, trod those lands, but there is no doubt that many of the modern swarms find railroads a valuable guide. Pliable had approached New York with that help, and now Timorous took advantage of another such artifact to reach first Atlanta, Georgia, and then Montgomery, Alabama. Confused by the city, Timorous and his fellows turned due west along the railroad. They went through Mississippi via Jackson and, still going west, came to the neighborhood of Dallas, Texas. West of Dallas they flew along the edge of the Edwards Plateau and turned southwest, the contours and winds taking them to Eagle Pass, a famous spot for butterfly migrations to and from Mexico and one, moreover, marked by man especially for Timorous with a railroad. On November 23 the swarm was a wonderful sight streaming through the pass on a gentle breeze and in bright sunlight, blazing in orange and velvety black; heedless of the border customs and emigration posts they flew on and landed for the night in Mexico, near Allende.

The following day Timorous kept to his southwest track, but soon the range of the Sierra Madre was facing him, so he and his companions turned southwest, as, partially, did the wind, and continued generally in that direction. The sun, though still sinking in the sky every day, was at a comforting height and the temperature at night was rising.[4] Ten days later they were on the edge of Lake Champayán, in the south of the Mexican state of Tamaulipas. Timorous found the weather warm and the sun at noon at the satisfactory level of 50 degrees over the horizon. It was December 4, and he was now in the tropics. He had covered a distance of about 2,000 miles as the crow flies (in point of fact crows do not fly dead straight from point to point) in 79 days, some 25 miles per day on an average. But he by no means traveled in a direct line. He had varied his direction considerably and had made many side trips to feed and to avoid obstacles and so had actually covered about 3,000 miles, or 38 miles per day. But he covered less distance than this at the start of his journey and much more per day at the end of it. Now the urge to travel faded and the butterflies took to their winter life—feeding, fluttering around the area, and mating.

Pliable was last noted at Roanoke Island. The thin spit of land from there leading down Hatteras Island to Cape Hatteras was not attractive to her so she turned southwest over Croatan Sound to

the mainland; keeping her direction she came to Bluff Point on
Pamlico Sound, almost open sea. She flew low. At one point over
this sea, exhaustion, confusion, and gusts of wind obliged her to
land on the water, along with many of her companions. Unless they
could get off fairly soon they would be lost. The rise from the
surface of a choppy sea is a considerable problem for a butterfly.
Apart from direct predators, such as fish and gulls, there are two
main dangers: the breaking wavelets might fracture a wing, and
the surface tension, or drag, of the water might prevent the insect
from flapping its wings fast enough to achieve flight.

Once on the water Pliable took remedial action. She rested a
little to regain her strength, rising and falling with the waves. The
waxy nature of her body chitin and the scales on her wings could
repel water for a while at any rate, but she would need oxygen. She
pressed her wings down on the water and raised her abdomen out
of it, thus insuring the circulation of air through the abdominal
spiracles and enabling her to keep up her strength. She would be
safe so long as her wings did not become water-soaked, a matter of
great importance. She could have lived, though weakly, a day or
more under water, the air already in her body just sufficing to
sustain life, but water-logged wings would be too heavy and could
not be moved fast enough to insure a take-off. The same problem
faces the airline pilot; if ice has accumulated on his craft's wings
it will be too heavy to rise.

Flying drops of spray beat on Pliable's wings, which water she
constantly shook off. She used the very waves and wind to help
her escape. Her sensitive antennae told her from which direction
the wind was coming, for she was no longer in the air, no longer
part of the wind. The breeze also drove the wavelets forward and
the rise and fall of the water gave her opportunities of mounting
in the air. There were two possibilities: The first was to face into

the wind, flap her wings as rapidly as she could, and use the wind to raise her quickly above the water, in the same way as an aircraft is helped to rise by taking off into the wind. The other possibility was to take off with the wind behind her, waiting until she was on the crest of a wave as it broke and then starting to flap her wings energetically. Although the breaking wavelet would then be dropping away from her, some droplets might also be carried forward with her, fall on her, and add to her weight. Pliable tried facing into the wind first; a wave raised her and just before it broke she lowered her abdomen into the water, beat her wings rapidly, and took off. But a gust of wind caught her and threw her back into a trough between the waves. The next time she was luckier; the trough between the crests was comparatively calm. Had she fallen into the breaking wave her wings could have been broken or become soaked, either of which would have been fatal. She shook off some flying spray and turned so that the wind was behind her. A wavelet raised her and she found she could see a few feet ahead. Rapidly she started flapping her wings over their full angle and took off just as the wave broke. She rose half an inch in the air; spray fell on her, but her rapid movements shook it off, so that her all-up weight was but momentarily increased, and she quickly gained height. Once more she was safe. Many of her companions, however, were lost to the waves. Pliable's success was largely due to good fortune and the fact that the stalling speed—the speed at which forward motion is lost and the creature or object merely drops under the force of gravity—is much less for a butterfly than for a bird and very much less than for an aircraft. The monarchs could be airborne at low speeds. The impulse given to Pliable by the breaking wave provided just the extra push needed to launch her into the air and safety, even though she was launched with the wind and thus got no such lift from it as she had tried to acquire on her first attempt. Only 4 feet up in the air she was part of it again, in an almost dead calm, a welcome change after the turbulence of the sea, although, in fact, she was moving with the wind, plus her own efforts, steadily southwest.

It is interesting to compare a monarch butterfly to a flying machine. No direct studies of this kind have been made on monarchs, but an English entomologist, Bernard Hocking, looked into the power requirements of some flies and bees; his findings have some bearing on the forces Pliable and Timorous needed. Hocking concluded that at low speeds the power needed for the support of the insect equals that required for its propulsion forward. At higher speeds the creature used more fuel per unit of distance covered.[5] Though men have known this for some time they have suddenly become far more conscious of it now that an energy crisis imposes a lower speed limit on motor cars. Both man and butterfly use less fuel per mile if they travel more slowly, perhaps a self-evident statement but also true for butterflies at comparatively low speeds. Insects are not particularly economical fliers, as a flapping wing to secure flight is not as efficient a device as a propeller or jet. Thomas Weis-Fogh, a Danish entomologist, worked out some comparative figures for aircraft and certain insects, expressing them as costs—in terms of kilo-calories per kilogram of the machine's and insect's weight per kilometer of distance flown. In effect, the amount of fuel used expressed as large calories.[6] He found that a small monoplane used 1 kilo-calorie per kilometer flown, a jet transport 2, a locust 5, and a bee 15 to 30. Their respective speeds were 300, 380, 4.5, and 10 to 20 miles per hour.

It is curious that such an apparently industrious creature as the bee should be so relatively inefficient. There are three points to bear in mind, though. For about half their flying time bees are

carrying back to the hive a considerable pay load of honey or
pollen, which naturally increases their fuel consumption. They fly
more quickly than the other insects studied, and bees care for and
feed their offspring. The monarchs let theirs fend for themselves.
Pliable and Timorous were more efficient fliers because they flew
more slowly, did not feed their young, and carried no loads, but
even so they had accumulated a weight of fat for use on their long
migration flights. It may be that bees need to be so industrious
just because they are relatively inefficient. In the scheme of nature
they have a near-monopoly of nectar exploitation in return for their
pollination activities, reminiscent of the monopoly power of a
strong trade union or a business consortium. Monopolists can
afford to be wasteful. Indigenous man in Central America is
another example; though highly civilized he was technically
inefficient in that he did not invent the wheel, the arch, or money.
There was no need to, because the native American plants—corn
and potatoes being the chief ones—gave him an easy livelihood.
Similarly the monarchs have a near-monopoly on milkweeds; they
are not subject to much competition from other forms of life.

The monarchs are also gliding experts, which again saves fuel;
they use wind power. Pliable and Timorous were constantly finding
rising air currents, using them to gain a little height and a view of
the surroundings and then dropping down among the flowers to
feed. An acre of open land produces about 1 ½ pounds of sugar in
the flowers per season, a considerable quantity for the monarchs.
Woodlands give only about a third as much; [7] a reason why trees
(except as roosts) were not popular with Pliable and Timorous and
their companions.

Pliable's and Timorous's wings as they flapped were not held
flat in one plane but were curved in various ways to give both
support—the downward push of the wing against the air—and a

backward thrust of the air to secure forward motion. Nor were the wings held exactly horizontal at midstroke. They were inclined one way or the other. The inclination of the wings was reversed at the end of each stroke, as must be the case if the two strokes (upward and downward) are not to cancel each other. Imagine Pliable's wings moving upward, with the trailing (rear) edge lower than the leading (forward) edge. The air is pushed up and back by the wing and she moves forward, dropping a fraction as she does so. At the top of the stroke the inclination of the wing is reversed; the wing goes down, pushing the air down and back, and Pliable is supported and pushed forward. The effect is simply to push the air back as does the propeller of an aircraft. It is as if an insect had two propellers directing a stream of air downward and backward, both keeping the creature up and moving it forward.[8] In a cruising flight Pliable moved her wings at a rate of about ten complete beats per second.

Still moving southwest, Pliable rose in the air, as did many of her surviving companions, and they were carried in that direction ahead of a cold front coming down the coast. After 30 miles of this she was once more over land and the butterflies roosted on the shores of New River Inlet, North Carolina. It was October 20. The night being stormy, Pliable sheltered with a number of companions, and as the storm continued the next day they did not venture afield but kept closely pressed together to ride it out. On October 21 the winds had abated, backing to the east. Pliable set off again on a southwest-by-west course for ten days, leading her inland over Columbia, South Carolina, where the rising land turned the wind, Pliable, and the swarm southwest. That diversion led them away from the route to Lighthouse Point, Florida, the place where so many monarchs congregate each winter. Even had Pliable reached that fashionable winter resort for her species it is doubtful if she would have been satisfied with it, for she, being of the same strain as Timorous, also liked a high winter sun. Not satisfied, like some of their kind, with a sun 37 degrees over the horizon at Christmas noon, they needed an angle of 50 degrees or 55 degrees on that day, as well as food, flowers, and warmth. Had Pliable reached Lighthouse Point, this need could well have carried her out over the Gulf of Mexico with a considerable possibility of death.

She continued southwest through Georgia, left the state at Columbus, and finally reached the coast again on the Gulf just west of New Orleans at Cameron, Louisiana. Here she turned along the coast and resumed her southwest track when the coast turned that way. She negotiated the narrow entrance to Galveston Bay successfully and followed the chain of the Texas coastal islands until it turned southeast. Keeping steadily on in a southwesterly direction, she crossed the Rio Grande and entered Mexico at Roma. As happened with Timorous, the Sierra Madre turned her south-southeast, and she too ended her journey at the shores of Lake Champayán. The date was December 18.

6 MEXICAN WINTER

DECEMBER 19 – MARCH 17

After Pliable arrived at Lake Champayán, her migratory instinct weakened and was succeeded by a developing mating instinct as she reached sexual maturity. Conditions around the lake were satisfactory, providing in abundance flowers, food, shelter, and male monarchs.

Timorous had been at the lakeside two weeks before Pliable reached there and had not yet found a mate. He would station himself on a leaf, keeping a sharp lookout. Once he chased a male monarch and once a female who did not respond to his advances. He had again made sallies after falling leaves and even after a hummingbird probing a tropical hibiscus flower—all failures and frustration. On January 12 he was still watching and waiting when Pliable flew by. Nothing daunted by previous mistakes, he set off in pursuit, stationing himself just ahead of and above her. Pliable, however, was in no hurry to mate; she had the rest of the winter before her. She took avoiding action, twisting and turning in her flight and dodging between leaves, but did not go into the ultimate antimale routine—the steady upward flight into the sky. Timorous, on the other hand, seemed convinced that this was the real thing at last—almost as if he had observed that both she and he had those strange white patches on the edges of their left forewings and therefore must be meant for each other. As a matter of fact, the patch helped him keep Pliable in sight. As she mounted in circles in the still air he followed, managing to keep in front of her most of the time. Finally, getting above her, he released his shower of scent and this time it worked. Pliable flew down and settled on a leaf, occasionally uncoiling her mouth as if she had merely set down there to feed. Timorous paraded beside her, opening and closing his wings as if to show what a splendid fellow he was. Pliable coiled up her mouth, turned away again, and flew off in a small circle. Timorous at once followed, got above, and again poured out his perfume, causing Pliable once more to settle and Timorous himself to restart his display, moving his wings slowly up and down and walking around Pliable. Next he drew up beside her, reinforcing his advantage by continually issuing his sex-lure scent. He then bent his abdomen sideways, making the end of it touch that of Pliable, who rejected his advances by curling her abdomen upward and opening and closing her wings. Timorous made another attempt, going through his display routine again, and this time Pliable remained quiet, with her wings closed. Timorous now firmly grasped Pliable's abdomen with his two powerful anal claspers, extruded his thin tubelike aedeagus and inserted it into Pliable's duct. A moment later the pair was frightened by a bird passing by. Timorous took to flight, still grasping Pliable by the end of her abdomen, and with great effort managed to fly with the female hanging beneath him.

The flight of coupled butterflies is naturally slower than and different from that of a single male or female. This pair happened to catch the eye of a Mexican entomologist who was watching the overwintering butterflies. He followed them with his powerful fieldglasses. After the bird had passed they settled on a tree branch about 6 feet above his head. The male—that is, Timorous—firmly grasped a twig with his two pairs of active legs. As the position they were in made it difficult to use his net the entomologist closed in on them; his fieldglasses, fitted with special extensions that enabled him to focus on objects as near as 6 feet, were invaluable for watching insects. He was astonished to discover that both butterflies bore labels, but try as he might he could see only the number and part of the address, Glens Falls, on the male. He wrote this information in his notebook. He next tried to capture the pair, but the disturbance he caused made Timorous take to flight again—his honeymoon twice disturbed at its critical moment. Timorous flew about a hundred yards and settled once more, this time in an open thicket and out of sight of the human observer.

Looked at objectively this mating is an amazing achievement. Pliable had her wings folded inside those of Timorous, which were also folded. The wing contact helped hold her in position, but her main support, as she hung with her head inclined downward, was from the firm hold of Timorous's anal claspers.

They remained in this position for an hour, during which time Timorous passed the spermatophore, a small bag containing his sperm, down his aedeagus into a special sac (the *bursa copulatrix*) in Pliable's abdomen. The sperm lodged there would remain viable for a long time and would be drawn on, little by little, as she laid her eggs.

After mating the two butterflies separated and both sought out flowers on which they fed.

THE YEAR OF THE BUTTERFLY

The Mexican observer, fascinated with his discovery, rushed into Tampico to find an atlas and locate Glens Falls. Using as an address "El Entomólogo, Glens Falls, N.Y., EE. UU. [United States]," he wrote at once, and in due course the young entomologist at Glens Falls received the letter—something of a triumph for the post-office intelligence system. The young couple, after they had found someone to translate the letter, rejoiced to learn that, after that long, long flight, one, and possibly two, of their specimens had been found. They wrote their thanks to their Mexican colleague.

Pliable now changed her habits and roosted with the other mated females and the males. She spent some weeks of leisurely life gliding among the tropical lakeside vegetation, feeding on flowers, converting the carbohydrates to fat in her body and ripening her eggs. Timorous, while continuing to feed, ripened further sperm within his body. He still felt the sex urge and on February 12 he mated with another female monarch.

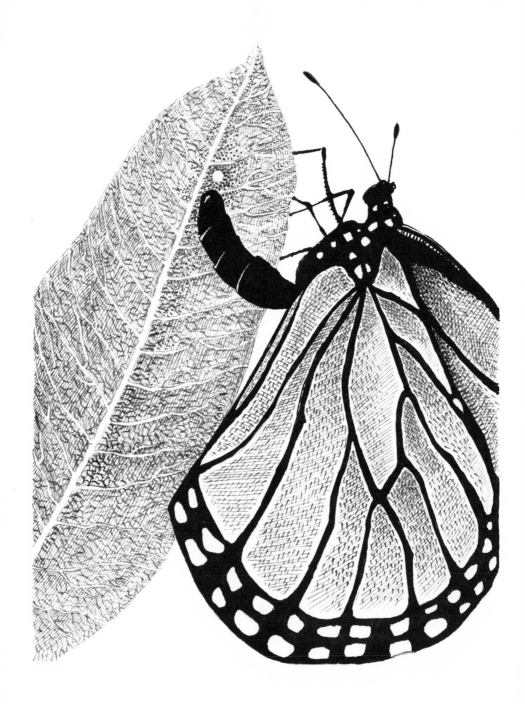

7 NORTHBOUND

MARCH 18–APRIL 30

By March 18 Pliable was aware that the sun was rising considerably higher in the sky each day, getting too high in fact. She was ready for egg-laying and the flowers were withering —food was running out, as well as her life span. Her migratory instinct took over again and she set off northward, away from the danger of too hot weather and dying milkweed plants.

The impulse to move north imposed itself on Timorous more gradually, but he finally set off on March 31, following the same route as that by which he had traveled south. Favorable winds took him along the escarpment of the Sierra Madre and once again he passed through Eagle Pass, this time in the opposite direction. In the pass itself strong gusts forced Timorous and his companions to take shelter on the lee side of some mesquite bushes. Many monarchs had their wings broken by the wind and fell to the ground, where they slowly died, but Timorous's luck held. He rode out the storm again and reached Texas the next day.

THE YEAR OF THE BUTTERFLY

The northward flight of Pliable, Timorous, and the other monarchs was more purposeful and direct than their southern one had been. Now they spent but little time in feeding. As they no longer chased from flower to flower for nectar but used their fat reserves as fuel, more time was available for the flight and for egg-laying by the females. In using their carefully accumulated fat reserves as fuel for their journey, however, they had to take in considerable quantities of water, for water is needed to convert the fat to energy. The monarchs get their water from dew, puddles, and raindrops. Successive chambers in the last part of the gut, as already mentioned, and special organs in the excretory system extract some of the water for reuse from the feces before these are voided. The water that butterflies use need not be particularly clean; they suck up with apparent relish urine, muddy water, and juices from decaying organic matter, no doubt extracting nourishment from these sources as well.

Pliable traveled north along the coast, crossing the Tropic of Cancer at Indios Morolanes Bay, keeping to the west side of the lagoon, where some fishermen cheered her on her way crying "¡Buen viaje, linda! [Good journey, pretty one!]." She continued along the west side of the long lagoon of the Madre Austral. Her eggs were developing rapidly. On the morning of March 25 she passed over a patch of grass and weeds on the outskirts of San Fernando, Tamaulipas. Her senses of sight and smell told her that the patch contained milkweed plants, and she began to look for suitable places for her eggs. She moved toward the milkweeds slowly, pushing out in front her first pair of legs, the almost useless ones, and flying up wind so as to reduce her speed of approach; she was almost hovering in the air. The two front legs held forward acted as shock absorbers, preventing her being driven against the plant by a sudden drop in the speed of a gust of wind. Perhaps this is why these so-called useless legs have survived—they seem to have a use in finding egg-laying sites.

Pliable used the greatest care in selecting just the right place to lay her eggs, for this was to be the sum total of her maternal solicitude. Once the eggs were laid, she would never see them again, nor would she see the caterpillars that hatched from them. Should she live long enough to meet a young adult from one of her early eggs, she would not know it as one of her own offspring. Nevertheless, it could be said that she took thought for the morrow of her children by choosing propitious places for them to hatch.

At this time of year she visited only young plants, about 6 inches high, and selected leaves of exactly the right color—the yellowish-green ones. By the time the caterpillar hatched, green or dark-green leaves would be too old and tough for the tiny jaws to penetrate.

Having chosen a leaf, she landed on it and tested it with the tarsi of her middle pair of legs, where her sense of taste lay. If the leaf was young, tender, and had the right taste (she had to avoid the poke milkweed), she then examined the underside. The down had to be soft and incipient; the young caterpillar, after eating its eggshell, would make its first meal on this down. Also the leaf had to be free of virus and other diseases: she could judge of virus disease by the yellow color of the tissues. She also had to avoid leaves infested with even a few greenflies; these insects could multiply enormously and crowd out the young hatchling from her egg. They could also infect the plant with the virus and dwarf it. These possibilities all had to be taken into account, for all or any of them could jeopardize the future of her offspring. She avoided leaves on which a monarch egg had already been laid; with so much leaf available there was no need for the young to have to compete for food by being crowded onto a leaf. Some kinds of butterflies deliberately lay their eggs in masses or in close proximity, finding that this enables the young to protect one another. On being frightened, all the young caterpillars in a concerted action will raise their heads and wave them from side to side: the movement repels certain predators. Since the monarchs are distasteful to many enemies, such action is not needed, and their solitary condition leads to a more efficient exploitation of the food available.

Pliable was particularly fussy about the site for her first egg; she rejected leaf after leaf on an open patch of milkweed. Some were too old, some too young; some were the wrong kind of plant; others were diseased or had greenfly or other insects on them; spiders were in evidence on others. Milkweeds were also growing among grasses which rose above them. Pliable noticed this and started crawling down a stem with her wings closed in order to try some lower leaves. It is not so much the wind gusts that batter and tear monarch wings; the searching for the proper place for the eggs and the crawling up and down grass stems cause the damage. The butterflies are part of the wind and move with it, but it can harm them in their roosts or when they are landing.

At last Pliable found a suitable leaf—the right shade of yellow-green, healthy, and with no insects on it. She settled on the upper side of the leaf and curled her abdomen around beneath it until the tip was in contact with the lower surface. To produce eggs Pliable had two ovaries, each composed of four ovarioles, and thus was more generously equipped than the human female, not surprisingly in view of the number of eggs she (Pliable) was going to produce—some 400. An ovariole consists of a long, thin tube in which the eggs are produced. The eggs pass down the ovariole into the oviduct and then into the vestibulum, or vagina. There they move in front of a passage leading from the second part of her sexual apparatus, the sperm store. The *bursa copulatrix* contains the sperm put into the female at copulation. A small quantity of

sperm is released as each egg passes in front of the passage from
the sperm sac. Some sperm penetrate each egg, though only one
sperm fertilizes each one. Most of Pliable's eggs were fertilized.
The egg, having received its dose of fertilizing sperm, was then
pushed out, base first. The base was covered with a sticky
substance, firmly cementing it to the underside of the leaf as
Pliable pushed it into the downy covering. At the same time she
marked the leaf with a special scented substance to warn other
female monarchs that this leaf already had an egg on it. She acted
quickly. Regaining the top surface of the leaf she climbed up the
grass stem, took off, flew a few yards, crawled down another grass
stem, and laid another egg on a suitable milkweed leaf.

After laying five eggs Pliable set off north again. She flew low
and rapidly. Every now and then milkweed plants in her path, as
well as the pressure of eggs in her body, caused her to pause and hunt
around for a suitable leaf for another egg. She first flew backward
and forward 6 inches above the milkweeds, giving the site a general
survey; if it appeared to be suitable she chose a leaf and landed on
it. Sometimes she was not quite sure of a leaf and would flutter
around it for some time, deliberately bumping into it with her
wings in order to drive off predators such as spiders, a mouse, or
even a fox.[1] Having laid eggs on different leaves, she would set off
again, using her full wing beat in a purposeful flight, in distinction
to the considerable amount of zooming, gliding, and hanging
around in the early stages of her southward journey. She overcame
obstacles in a different way too: she now flew up and over a
building in her path, coming down again to her previous level when
she had passed it, whereas on the southward journey she had
turned left or right to fly around buildings. The more earnest
migrants, such as those in the northward flight, seem less inclined
to give up their set track. Once again Pliable usually roosted alone,

this time because there were far fewer survivors flying north than had set off southward in the fall. The butterflies were nothing like so conspicuous.

Pliable passed over the Rio Grande at its mouth, just west of Bagdad, Texas. There the winds took her inland to Alice, where she was able to resume the northeast track by now imprinted on her brain. She crossed the Colorado River at Lagrange, and at Hearne picked up the railroad running northeast. Using this as a guide she turned east at Marshall, keeping along the railroad by way of Vicksburg and Meridian, Mississippi, to Atlanta, Georgia. Here she turned northeast along the base of the Appalachian Mountains to return to Baltimore.

All the way along she had been laying eggs at the rate of about ten per day. Now the *bursa* was empty, her colors were faded and her wings torn, though the label was still bravely attached. Her fuel reserves of fat had all been used. Nectar was available once more and she fed from time to time on that. The emptying of her *bursa* led to a slight reawakening of her sex urge and she hunted around in a desultory way for a male monarch, but her heart was not really in the search. But her ovarioles were still working. She looked for suitable milkweed leaves, still using great care to get just the right one, and laid some final eggs. These were all infertile because her *bursa* could not supply the sperm to activate them. She never knew that they would not hatch.

8 JOURNEY'S END

MAY 1–8

Pliable laid her last three infertile eggs at Timberlane on
May 1. Then she was caught by a gust of wind and blown
against a thorn bush, breaking the leading edge of her forward
left wing, which was already rather tattered. She fell to the ground,
fluttering helplessly. As she struggled to rise, she became more and
more exhausted. A scouting ant came across her, felt her body with
its feelers, and hurried back to the nest with the news of a fine
protein meal in the offing. Sensing danger, Pliable managed to
flutter a few inches away, so that when the scout returned with a
gang of workers the promised treat could not be found. The
butterfly lay in the middle of a small path through a wood. Try as
she would she could not rise; she had no fat left and there was no
water in reach. What little water reserves she had were being
drained by the dry early summer weather. In the air above her she
could see the bright young monarchs flying purposefully by,
moving steadily north to occupy their territory all the way into

Canada. They were the successors that would maintain the status quo, that would prevent the milkweeds from dominating the earth, a task in which the monarchs are far more effective than any herbicide used by man.

As Pliable lay on the path, scarcely able to move, another ant scout found her and took the news back to the nest. This time the scout was able to lead the work force back to the butterfly. They started to swarm over her. Pliable tried to release her ant-repellent substance but was too exhausted to do so. The ants knew just what to do; rapidly their sharp jaws started to bite through the wing tendons to the body. Pliable beat her wings and twisted her body, managing to move a few inches, but some ants clung to her. When she came to rest, other ants caught up with her. Soon they had cut off her wings from her body. Now, helpless, she died, her long journey done.

Motivated by the need to secure food, and thus the survival and increase of the species, she had traveled some 3,500 miles over the United States and Mexico. There had been pleasures in her life, such as gliding in the warm September sunlight in a land full of plenty and being rewarded for her arduous flight from the north by similar comforts in the mild coastal Mexican winter. These, however, were but preparations for her main task of propagating her species, and that she had achieved. In addition, she had derived satisfaction from finding just the right spot for each of her eggs. Even now some of her first offspring were finding their wings and soon would be setting off northward.

The ants carefully cut up Pliable's body and took the pieces back to their nest. The wings, of no interest to them, were left on the path. On May 2 a boy walking through the woods found the faded wings and, intrigued by the label, sent them back to the address given. The young couple at Glens Falls were delighted to have yet another recovery, setting a time if not a distance record. Pliable had been labeled on September 12 and the wings, found on May 2, were reasonably fresh and could not have been lying on the ground for long. The girl maintained that No. GF.2575, like GF.2580, had been to Mexico and thus was on her way back, but there was no evidence for this, and the young man, to annoy her, plumped for the view that the butterfly had spent the winter in a hollow tree at Stevenson—a heresy of the first order.

Timorous, last mentioned at Eagle Pass, continued steadily northeastward; he moved somewhat faster than Pliable because he did not have to pause to lay eggs. At Houston, Texas, he got a fixation on the railroad and turned east. He was using up his fat reserve at a rapid rate, and on the banks of the Mississippi River he started to take nectar from the spring flowers in order to extend his range. He then kept along the coast until he reached Pensacola, Florida. Here he turned northeast and soon joined with the swarms from Lighthouse Point, now coming north on their return flight. Most of the females had mated, had their *bursae* full, and were not interested in any advances he made to them.

As far as the monarch race was concerned, Timorous had done his duty; he had mated twice. It could not matter much whether he continued north or not; he was no longer essential, as were the females. It could not matter *much*; it might matter a little. He could be a pathfinder for a swarm; he could help provide protection at night for a roosting colony. If he fell a victim to a predacious bird, his fate would teach it a lesson by causing it to vomit and, by giving the bird an aversion to monarchs, save the lives of pregnant females in his company. Moreover, he might mate again on his journey with one of the new-generation females arising along the way. Also his great experience in flying enabled him to select good overnight sites. It was as if he knew that the roost was of the greatest importance and that it was wise to select this as the sun was setting, instead of flying later into the evening. It was better to lose distance than to have an unsafe refuge. This knowledge was simply part of his makeup. Though Timorous might not always be at the head of his stream, when he selected a roost many of his companions joined him. They always came through, whereas those that covered a greater distance and roosted at the last minute were often destroyed by storms or predators during the night. The timorous butterflies were being more successful than the bold. Timorous's descendants were likely to inherit some characteristics most useful to succeeding monarch generations: long-distance flying ability and skill in finding good roosting sites.

The monarchs are a successful species in that the circumstances of their lives can allow a male past his age of major utility to continue to live, consume food and living space, and to be of minor service to the community. They thus resemble man; most human races allow the old to live. It is to be hoped that, in spite of human population pressure, circumstances will continue to permit this for some time to come.

Coming up the South Carolina coast Timorous began to lose strength. On May 8 the wind took him and some of his companions out to sea in Long Bay. As the wind from the southeast freshened, he came down low into the boundary layer to reduce his speed, but at the entrance to the channel between Smith Island and Southport, North Carolina, a wave caught him and swept him into the sea. He managed to get to the surface again, but his wings soon became water-soaked and he drowned. His body was washed up on the sands at Myrtle Beach, but no one found it or his label; both were gradually ground into the sand.

JOURNEY'S END

On May 1, the day Pliable died, Pliable II/I emerged as an adult from her pupal case, at San Fernando, Tamaulipas, as did also a number of her brothers and sisters. With the warm weather and high sun she soon set off north, taking the coastal route.

9 SUCCEEDING GENERATIONS

MAY 9 – AUGUST 7

In the warm summer weather all along the migration route the monarchs developed more quickly. Pliable II/I mated in Texas on May 12, laid her eggs in the Carolinas and Maryland between May 16 and June 1, and died from exhaustion in Pennsylvania on June 2, having given rise to the third generation. Pliable III/I, hatched on May 18, also matured quickly, emerging as an adult on June 25. She too was soon moving northward and laying eggs. On July 15 she fell from a low roost and was eaten by a shrew. Pliable IV/I, emerging as an adult on July 25, joined the northbound flight.

The drive to move north was persistent. The monarchs stopped going forward only when the milkweeds in an area they had reached were not sufficiently advanced, or when the weather was against them. They sheltered among shrubs in bad weather, and if the milkweeds they found in a new zone were not in a suitable state for egg-laying (that is, only just budding with no young leaves), they would cruise up and down, feeding on open blossom of all kinds, waiting until the milkweeds were ready, with the females persistently searching for suitable ones all the time. Thus they adjusted their northward movement in accordance with the state of the milkweeds, which in turn depended on the weather. The monarchs usually arrived at their food plants when these were just right for the first eggs, and ahead of most of the few other insects that can use the plant.

The overlapping of the generations meant that at any spot along the route caterpillars of all sizes could be found on the milkweeds, and old, faded, and torn butterflies could be seen floating among bright fresh new ones. The summer generations are very short compared with the long, overwintering fall generation.

As June turned to July the urge to move north began to fade and the adult monarchs seemed to find time to enjoy life once more. The potential increase of monarchs is enormous, with each female producing 200 more females three or four times a year, but the swarms, though varying in numbers a little from year to year and seeming to reach a peak every seven years, do not get out of hand and extinguish the milkweed, the only plant on which the young can feed. Various factors limit a runaway increase, two main ones being a virus disease of the caterpillars and the difficulty of finding suitable egg sites.

Diseased caterpillars turn black and die and can infect their fellows. As to the egg sites, the exacting standards of the female monarchs have been described. On the unusual occasions when, because of overcrowding, an egg is laid on a leaf which already has one on it, the first caterpillar to hatch will eat the other egg, as Timorous did, thus helping in population control in overproductive years.

SUCCEEDING GENERATIONS

In July the Glens Falls entomologist and student married and, intrigued by the example of the monarchs, went to visit their Mexican correspondent at Lake Champayán for their honeymoon. When they returned home on August 7 they found new monarch eggs on the leaves of their milkweed patch. Some of these, although the couple had no way of knowing it, had been laid that morning by Pliable IV/I; the cycle was beginning again.

The monarchs fill an important ecological niche in the economy of our interrelated natural world; they prevent its complete domination by a particular plant. They eat down the milkweed so that it remains just another reasonably abundant American plant, and not a devastating swamping weed. The public monuments to the monarchs' beauty are the butterfly trees of such places as Pacific Grove, California, and Lighthouse Point, Florida. Here, winter after winter, these butterflies mysteriously gather in a blaze of winter color—a much admired tourist attraction protected by law. The monarchs' true monument is the beautiful American countryside with its trees, flowers, and grasses that their lives and appetites have saved from submersion in a choking sea of green, poisonous milkweeds.

APPENDIXES
REFERENCE NOTES
CHRONOLOGY
GLOSSARY
SELECTED BIBLIOGRAPHY
INDEX

APPENDIX I:
Anthropomorphism

An author writing for a nontechnical audience is frequently obliged to use forms and similes which fill any scientific friends left to him with horror, in case he should be guilty of the crime of anthropomorphism. Animals frequently appear to act as if motivated by human reasoning, and though the apparent anthropomorphist knows quite well that this is not the case he may well draw attention to the similarity by using words that might appear anthropomorphic. In this way he avoids the tedious repetition of such phrases as "appeared to think" and "seemed to act as if" at the same time that he indicates parallel lines of conduct between man and animal. One feels he may be in good company. C. B. Williams, the English authority on insect migration, discussing the end of a flight, asks, "Has the sex instinct developed and overpowered or inhibited the migration instinct, or do the butterflies say, more or less figuratively, 'Here is the promised land, to which we have fought our way to provide for our offspring, and here we will stay!'?" I like his phrase "more or less." He then makes amends for his crime by saying: "To put the latter a little more seriously, does the presence of abundant food plants and climatic conditions suitable for the offspring bring about any physiological change that suppresses the mating instinct?" [1]

Edward Gibbon, the eighteenth-century English historian of the Roman Empire, in what is at first sight a startling phrase, reports that Saint Augustine was "scandalized by the anthropomorphism of the vulgar." [2] It would be surprising if the vulgar knew what the word meant, but they could well have been anthropomorphic in the saint's eyes without being aware of it. What scandalized Augustine undoubtedly was an anthropomorphism toward the Deity rather than in connection with animals.

The second sentence of the present book reads "Plants fight back." I am not suggesting that plants consciously organize themselves into defense corps, appointing some species as infantry and others as artillery and air forces, though all these branches could be said to exist among them. The "infantry" creep forward on the top of or just underneath the ground by means of stolons (underground shoots, becoming roots) thus advancing the territory occupied by the species in question. The "artillery" are plants such as peas with dehiscent seed pods that burst when ripe and shoot the seeds out. Airborne seeds are common. Such devices are used more in the struggle among species of plants than in that of plants against animals. Some plants actually feed on animals, entirely or partially. Ringworm is caused by funguses growing on the skin of animals and humans. The pitcher plants (*Sarracena* species) attract insects, drown them in the pitchers of the flowers, and there digest them, in addition to growing in the ordinary way by using elements drawn from the soil and the air. The Venus's fly trap (*Dionaea musicipula*) literally traps flies and digests them. These mechanisms are actually for feeding rather than defense, however. What happens there is that tiny variations in the offspring of plants that give some protection against animals enable these plants to survive at the expense of plants without such advantages, and hence the protective devices become established over a number of generations. This is the very essence of Darwinism. The holly bush has thorns on the leaves because a chance variation of a prickly leaf at some distant point in the past gave such prickly plants a better chance of surviving, until, as time went on, only the prickly-leaved plants were produced. It is interesting to note that the upper leaves of a tall holly bush have few or no prickles, presumably because they have not been exposed to attack from animals tall enough to reach them. A plant may develop irritant spines or hairs to deter animals from touching it.

The development of poisons in plants is another defense mechanism, as is also the presence of bad-tasting substances in the foliage. As the generations went on, the struggle between plants and animals continued. The animals with a tendency to leave the poisonous plants alone survived and at the same time encouraged the production and survival of the poisonous plant. The plant thus appears to have driven off the animal and the animal to have learned to avoid the dangerous plant. That is not exactly the case (although it is a recent heresy known as Lysenkoism), because the characteristics in the plant of developing poisonous foliage, and in the animal of avoiding it, were mostly present in the original germ plasm of both plant and animal and have been selected out. (Please notice the word "mostly"; some variations in plants and animals over the ages may have resulted from mutations, such mutations being largely induced by radiation activity.)

A common example of a poisonous plant is the pretty foxglove (*Digitalis purpurea*), and it is surprising that more children are not poisoned by this. The reason is that besides being poisonous it has a nasty taste. If mammals or children take a mouthful they promptly spit it out. Strangely enough, poisons in plants can cause addiction in certain animals and man. Cattle that have recovered from yew poisoning sometimes develop a craving for yew, break out of their pastures to seek it, and again poison themselves. Man can become addicted to the poisons in certain plants in spite of the harm they do him; examples are cocaine, marijuana, and tobacco. Because of this fact, the last-mentioned obscure American weed has come to be cultivated on a vast scale (over 8 million acres a year) all over the world. Its particular poison has led to its becoming more successful—that is, to cover a bigger area—as a crop than it would have covered if it had taken its chance in the wild.

Animals in their turn appear to fight back. The animal kingdom is vast and diversified, and plants which are poisonous to some are not at all so to others. There may be exceptions within a family; for instance, the death cap fungus (*Amanita phalloides*) is highly poisonous to man and most mammals but not to the rabbit. However, such cases are not common. Large numbers of the lower animals, particularly insects, have adapted themselves to feeding on poisonous plants, for here was a field open to exploitation. The milkweeds (*Asclepias* species) are a case in point. They are poisonous and are avoided by browsing animals, and the push and pull of evolution has led the monarch butterflies and a few other insects to colonize this splendid source of food.

Plants do have a major use for some animals—as pollinators. A condition of mutual help exists between them, the state known as symbiosis. In return for cross fertilization the plant provides food—nectar and pollen—and often displays strikingly colored and shaped signals, its flowers, to attract particular creatures such as bees, butterflies, and hummingbirds to its sexual parts. This secures the transference of the pollen of one flower to the stigma of another, leading to the crossing of lines, variation in the offspring, the accumulation of characteristics favorable to the survival and spread of the species, and the extinction of unfavorable lines. Plants also use animals to distribute their seeds.[3]

APPENDIX II:
Population Control

The superfamily of insects called the Ichneumonoidea is of great importance. All its members are all parasitic on other insects or other arthropods (jointed-limbed animals, including spiders and millipedes, and other creatures similar to, but not insects, strictly speaking) and are consequently toward the end of food chains. As such they do much to prevent an inordinate increase of insects, for without some such mechanism the animal life of the world would consist of insects and very little else. The reproductive power of insects is enormous. A female monarch butterfly will lay 400 eggs which on hatching will yield some 200 females and 200 males. Four generations a year are not uncommon, so that if all the larvae survived and reached maturity, one pair of monarchs would give rise to $2\,(200^4) = 3,200$ million butterflies in one year and they would weigh about 13,000 tons. At this rate the world would be knee deep in monarchs in a very short time. Many insects lay far more than 400 eggs and have correspondingly greater reproduction potentials. It is obvious that insects do not increase at that rate. The loss on the way is severe, and the dangers to monarchs in particular are discussed in the text. Hymenopterous insects and certain parasitic flies (Diptera) do much to prevent this population explosion, as do also diseases, lack of food, and scarcity of appropriate sites for the eggs.

A high fecundity is by no means essential for the production of an enormous population. The fact that animals produce more offspring than the environment can support was one of the considerations that led Charles Darwin to formulate his theory of the survival of the fittest and write his great work *On the Origin of Species by Means of Natural Selection*. The example of geometrical progression he gave was the slow breeding elephant. He wrote:

"The elephant is reckoned the slowest breeder of all known animals, and I have taken some pains to estimate its probable minimum rate of natural increase; it will be safest to assume that it begins breeding when thirty years old, and goes on breeding till ninety and surviving till one hundred years old; if this be so, after a period of from 740 to 750 years there would be nearly nineteen million elephants alive, descended from the first pair." [1]

The increase is considerably slower than that of the monarch, but just as inevitable. Those given to idle speculation, such as myself, may thus debate whether a world populated by monarchs of the insect kind or by elephants would be more desirable, driving one inevitably to an almost Panglossian acceptance of things more or less as they are rather than either of the alternatives mentioned.

The fundamental difference between the insect and the human worlds is that in the former population explosions are prevented by a tremendous wastage—a high death rate, particularly among the young—whereas in the human world we at least know that it is better to reduce births rather than to eliminate the surplus population by wars and pogroms. Not that wars (unless with hydrogen bombs) are much good at reducing population. During World War II the life expectation of an eighteen-year-old youth considerably increased, because in the army he received medical attention he could not have afforded in civilian life. This more than compensated for the deaths caused by warfare; it reduced the average death rate. At some future point, if we are not prepared to reduce our birth and/or survival rates, we must return to the natural system—premature killing of the population by famine, disease, predation, and parasitism. However, one does need to get a little proportion into this concept. It used to be said that the population of the world could stand shoulder to shoulder on Martha's Vineyard and there are times on a sunny summer Sunday when one thinks that this strange event is happening, if not actually completed. Alas! The world population is now too large for this to be done. Perhaps it is some consolation to know that they could at least stand on Rhode Island and would weigh 150 million tons.

The enormous fecundity of insects is one reason that chemical pest control is fundamentally unsatisfactory, except to the manufacturer of pesticides. A modern spray may kill 99.5 percent of the pest invasion, but the 0.5 percent left will rapidly build up the population again to normal and the spraying will have to be repeated several times a year season after season. In the future farmers will inevitably come to rely more on ichneumons and less on chemicals; for one thing the former are much cheaper. Insecticides are, of course, much less cruel than ichneumons, which is perhaps a point in their favor. To die from a paralysis of the nervous system induced by DDT one would imagine would be more or less painless, whereas to have your entrails slowly eaten out by an ichneumon larva sounds most unpleasant, though how much the caterpillar suffers we do not know. Parasitized caterpillars are active and feed well, often eating more than unparasitized ones, as they have their parasites to feed as well.

The early naturalists were frequently struck with this harsh mechanism of population reduction and, somewhat anthropocentrically, were wont to attribute it to divine intervention. The two nineteenth-century English clergymen, William Kirby and William Spence, whose *Introduction to Entomology* did much to popularize the science, in describing the attack of the cabbage white caterpillar and its reduction by parasites, wrote:

"And if we compare the myriads of caterpillars that often attack our cabbage and brocoli [*sic*] with the small number of butterflies of this species which usually appear, we may conjecture that they are commonly destroyed in some such proportion—a circumstance that will lead us thankfully to acknowledge the goodness of Providence, which by providing such a check has prevented the utter destruction of the Brassica genus, including some of our most esteemed vegetables." [2]

What the two learned clergymen had not realized was that many species of plants and animals in the past had suffered just that fate and today are known only as fossils. We see only the survivors of the holocaust.

The great proliferation of offspring allows those with some advantage over their fellows to survive. This is how the leopard got its spots and how the monarch came to do many things that other butterflies could not, such as feeding on a poisonous plant with impunity, acquiring a bad taste by accumulating those poisons in its body, displaying warning colors and long waving tentacles, and developing a pattern of migration. In fact, the monarch seems to have so many survival factors in its favor that it is surprising that the world is not knee deep in them.

REFERENCE
NOTES

CHAPTER 1

1. Samuel H. Scudder, *Brief Guide to the Common Butterflies of the Northern United States and Canada* (New York: Henry Holt & Co., 1893), and *The Life of the Butterfly: The Monarch* (New York: Henry Holt & Co., 1893).
2. Scudder, *Life of a Butterfly*.
3. Roger Caillois, *Méduse et Cie* (Paris, Gallimard, 1960); English translation by George Ordish, *The Mask of Medusa* (New York: Clarkson N. Potter; London: Victor Gollancz, 1964).

CHAPTER 2

1. F. A. Urquhart, *The Monarch Butterfly* (Toronto: University of Toronto Press, 1960), p. 38.

CHAPTER 3

1. Thomas Mouffet, *The Theatre of Insects*, trans. Edward Topsell (London, 1658), p. 958.

REFERENCE NOTES

2. *L'Encyclopédie* (Neufchâtel, France, 1721–1779), Vol. XI, p. 872.
3. Frank Cowan, *Curious Facts in the History of Insects* (Philadelphia: Lippincott, 1865), p. 396.
4. H. W. Bates, "Contributions to an Insect Fauna of the Amazon Valley. Lepidoptera: Heliconides," *Transactions Linnean Society* 23 (1862); and *The Naturalist on the River Amazon* (London: Murray, 1863).
5. *Encyclopaedia Britannica*, XV, p. 487.
6. D. F. Owen, *Tropical Butterflies* (Oxford: Clarendon Press, 1971), pp. 132–134; and chapter 9.
7. F. M. Jones, "Insect Coloration and the Relative Susceptibility of Insects to Birds. *Transactions of the Entomological Society of London* 80 (1932): 345–386.
8. Quoted in "Monarch Butterfly vs Blue Jay," *Insect World Digest*, March/April 1973, pp. 18–20.
9. Caillois, *The Mask of Medusa*, pp. 65, 71, 74.
10. Colette, *Journal de Rebours*, quoted in D. Matthews, *The Pursuit of Moths* (London: Chatto and Windus, 1957), p. 27.
11. E. N. Cory, "Monarch Butterfly," *Insect Pest Survey Bulletin* 14 (Washington, D.C., 1934).

CHAPTER 4

1. Charles G. Johnson, *Migration and Dispersal of Insects by Flight* (London: Methuen, 1969), p. 98; Thomas Weis-Fogh, "Weight Economy of Flying Insects," *Transactions IX Congress on Entomology, Amsterdam, 1951* (Amsterdam, 1952), Vol. I, pp. 341–347.
2. Weis-Fogh, "Weight Economy of Flying Insects."
3. Caillois, *The Mask of Medusa*, pp. 90–97.
4. Johnson, *Migration and Dispersal* . . . , p. 131.
5. *Ibid.*, p. 133.
6. G. C. T. Matthews, *Bird Migration* (London: Collins, 1948).
7. Walter Sullivan, "Monarchs in Hordes Heading South," *New York Times*, October 2, 1973.

8. "Swarms of Butterflies," *Cleveland Plain Dealer*, September 20, 1892, p. 8.

CHAPTER 5

1. Vincent E. Wigglesworth, *The Life of Insects* (London: Weidenfeld and Nicolson, 1964), p. 198.
2. Scudder, *Brief Guide . . . ,* p. 56; George Bentham and James D. Hooker, *Handbook of the British Flora*, 7th ed. (Ashford, Kent, England: L. Reeve, 1947), p. 297.
3. W. J. Holland, *The Butterfly Book* (New York: Doubleday, 1918), p. 297.
4. J. Rzedowski, "Nota sobre un vuelo migratorio de la mariposa *Danaus plexippus* L. observada en la región de Ciudad del Maíz," *Acta Mexicana Zoológica*, II, no. 2, pp. 1–4, March 1957.
5. Bernard Hocking, "On the Intrinsic Range and Speed of Flight of Insects," *Transactions Royal Entomological Society of London*, 104 (1953), 225–250.
6. Weis-Fogh, "Weight Economy of Flying Insects."
7. Hocking, "On Intrinsic Range and Speed," p. 250.
8. A. D. Imms, *A General Textbook of Entomology* (London: Methuen, 1934), p. 159.

CHAPTER 7

1. Edwin Way Teale, *Grassroots Jungles* (New York: Dodd Mead, 1937), p. 41.

APPENDIX I

1. C. B. Williams, *Insect Migration* (London: Collins, 1965), p. 392.
2. Edward Gibbon, *The History of the Decline and Fall of the Roman Empire* (London: Strahan and Cadell, 1788), Vol. IV, p. 540.
3. J. B. Free, *Insect Pollination of Crops* (New York: Academic Press, 1970).

REFERENCE NOTES

APPENDIX II

1. Charles Darwin, *On the Origin of Species by Means of Natural Selection* (London: J. Murray, 1859), pp. 78–90.
2. William Kirby and William Spence, *An Introduction to Entomology or Elements of the Natural History of Insects* (London: Longman, 1818), pp. 269–270.

CHRONOLOGY

August   8   Monarch eggs laid at Glens Falls, New York
        10   Caterpillars Pliable and Timorous hatch
        12   Pliable's first molt
        13   Timorous's first molt
        14   Pliable's second molt
        15   Timorous's second molt
        20   Pliable's third molt
        22   Timorous's third molt
        26   Pliable's fourth molt
        29   Timorous's fourth molt
             Pliable pupates

September 1   Timorous pupates
         12   Pliable emerges as adult; is captured, labeled,
             and released; flies to Hudson Falls, New York
         14   Timorous emerges as adult
         15   Pliable at Albany, New York
         16   Timorous is captured, labeled, and released

CHRONOLOGY

THE YEAR OF THE BUTTERFLY

June 2   Pliable II/I dies in Pennsylvania
     25   Pliable III/I emerges as adult
     29   Pliable III/I starts laying eggs

July 15   Pliable III/I dies
     25   Pliable IV/I emerges as adult

August 7   Pliable IV/I lays eggs at Glens Falls, New York

GLOSSARY

aedeagus:

the male organ of the adult butterfly.

anal clasper:

the last (rearward) pair of prolegs (false legs) of caterpillars; used to hold tightly to supports, such as leaf edges and stems, particularly when molting.

androconia:

specialized scales found on the wings of some male butterflies. They give off a scent attractive to the females of the species.

azimuth:

a concept used in astronomy and navigation; the angular distance the arc of a circle makes with a meridian. If a line is dropped from the apparent position of the sun in the sky to the horizon the angle that such a point makes with the north pole and the

	observer is the azimuth of the sun at that moment.
Batesian mimicry:	imitation, by a butterfly whose taste appeals to birds, of the appearance of a bad-tasting species, presumably to gain some protection.
boundary layer:	layer of air near the ground, in which wind moves more slowly.
bursa copulatrix:	a special receptacle inside the female butterfly which receives sperm during copulation and stores it. Later as the eggs pass down the vagina for oviposition sperm is directed to them from the *bursa copulatrix;* some sperm enter the egg by the micropyles and fertilize it.
chitin:	a hard flexible substance forming the exoskeleton of insects.
chrysalis:	the shell or case into which caterpillars turn when fully grown and from which the adult or imago (butterfly or moth) emerges; the pupa. It is frequently gold-colored and is named from the Greek word for gold.
corpus allatum:	the gland at the back of an insect's head secreting the *juvenile hormone* which holds back pupation. When production of this hormone ceases, by direction of the brain, the insect pupates.
cremaster:	the organ of attachment of the chrysalis or pupa, usually a hard knob with some hooks, on the hind segment.

138

GLOSSARY

cuticle: the outermost layer of the skin of insects

esophagus: part of the alimentary canal, leading from the mouth to the intestines

exarate pupa: *see* pupa

exoskeleton: the skeleton of insects, which is external; there is no internal framework as in vertebrates.

galeae: part of the maxilla, or jaws, of an insect. In the Lepidoptera (butterflies and moths) the galeae are greatly developed during pupation and become the coiled, sucking mouth by which the adult feeds, except in a few species which, as adults, do not feed at all.

hibernaculum: a wintering place. A caterpillar may form a hibernaculum by manipulating a leaf in a way that will cause a shelter for the winter to form.

instar: a period in an insect's life between molts. The first instar is the period between hatching and the first molt; the second instar is between the first and second molts; the third instar is between the second and third molts; the fourth instar is between the third and fourth molts; the fifth instar is between the fifth molt and pupation; the sixth instar is the pupa, and the seventh is the adult, or imago. Not all insects have seven instars.

Lepidoptera: an order of insects having wings covered with scales, the butterflies and moths.

139

Malpighian tubes: special organs in the abdomen of
                      insects which extract waste products
                      from the blood, sending them to the
                      hind gut for excretion.

maxilla: the jaw of an insect; *see* galeae.

meconium: the drops of semiliquid waste products
                      accumulated during pupation and
                      discharged shortly after emergence of
                      the adult butterfly.

mesothorax: *see* thorax.

metathorax: *see* thorax.

micropyle: a special pore situated at the top of
                      the monarch egg, through which
                      sperm is admitted to fertilize the egg.

obtect pupa: *see* pupa.

ocellus (pl., ocelli):   simple eye, or eyes, of insects; also the
                      eye spots seen on the wings of some
                      butterflies.

prolegs: the false legs of a caterpillar on the
                      abdomen, as distinguished from the
                      true legs on the thorax.

prothorax: *see* thorax.

pupa: the quiescent stage of an insect; in the
                      case of the monarch the chrysalis stage
                      between caterpillar and adult. In an
                      exarate pupa the wings and legs are
                      not attached to the body; in a semi-
                      exarate pupa furrowlike lines are visible;
                      in an obtect pupa (the later monarch
                      form) the appendages are firmly
                      attached.

GLOSSARY

retinal image:
: the picture received by the insect from its eyes. The retinal image tends to regulate speed and direction of flight.

sclerotin:
: a tough substance found in the skin of insects, particularly useful in hardening certain parts, such as the jaws.

spiracle:
: one of a series of small apertures through which air is admitted to the breathing tubes of insects; *see* tracheae.

striae:
: the tiny lines and ridges on the scales of butterfly wings. The striae break up the light and cause refraction colors on the wings.

tarsus (pl., tarsi):
: a section of the legs of insects, roughly corresponding to the bones of the flat part of the human foot.

thorax:
: the middle of the three regions of an insect's body, divided into three sections: prothorax (forward section), mesothorax (middle section), and metathorax (rear section). In the adult monarch a pair of true legs is attached to each section, the prothoracic legs not being much used. The wings arise from the mesothorax and metathorax.

tracheae:
: the breathing tubes by which oxygen is diffused through the bodies of insects, which have no lungs; *see* spiracle.

vestibulum:
: the sexual passage of the adult female butterfly.

SELECTED
BIBLIOGRAPHY

Caillois, Roger. *Medusa et Cie.* Illustrated. Paris: Gallimard, 1960. English translation by George Ordish, *The Mask of Medusa.* New York: Clarkson N. Potter; London: Victor Gollancz, 1964.

Cowan, Frank. *Curious Facts in the History of Insects.* Philadelphia: Lippincott, 1865.

Johnson Charles G. *Migration and Dispersal of Insects by Flight.* London: Methuen, 1969.

Kirby, William, and Spence, William. *An Introduction to Entomology or Elements of the Natural History of Insects.* London: Hunt, Rees, Orme, and Brown, 1818.

Mouffet, Thomas. *The Theatre of Insects.* Translated by Edward Topsell. London, 1658.

Owen, D. F. *Tropical Butterflies.* Oxford: Clarendon Press, 1971.

Scudder, Samuel H. *Brief Guide of the Common Butterflies of the Northern United States and Canada.* New York: Henry Holt & Co., 1893.

SELECTED BIBLIOGRAPHY

Scudder, Samuel H. *The Life of a Butterfly*. New York: Henry Holt & Co., 1893.

Urquhart, F. A. *The Monarch Butterfly*. Toronto: University of Toronto Press, 1960.

Wigglesworth, Vincent E. *The Life of Insects*. London: Weidenfeld and Nicolson, 1964.

Williams, C. B. *Insect Migration*. London: Collins, 1965.

INDEX

INDEX

INDEX

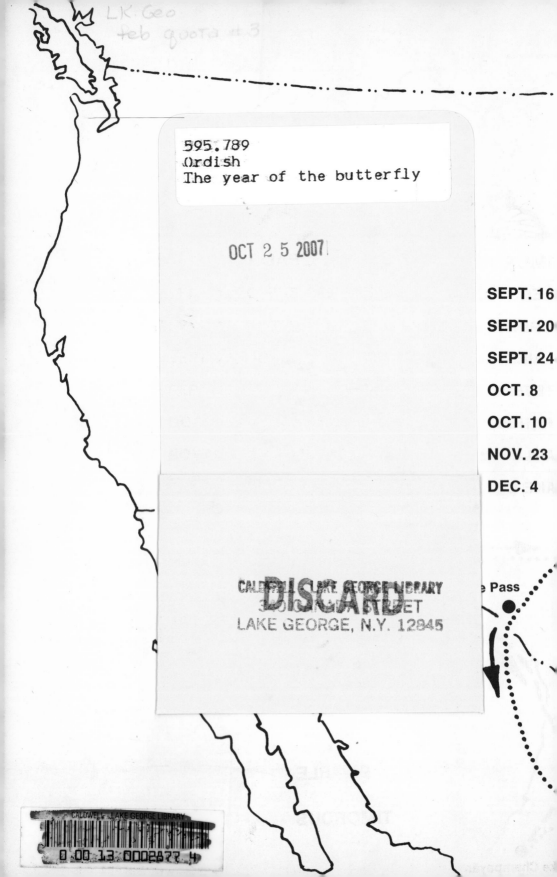

e Pass